What People Are

Enlarging t..

It's a delight to get to know two such faithful and thoughtful Friends as Nim Njuguna and Jonathan Doering through this wide-ranging and profound set of conversations that explore what Friends and others may be able or perhaps ought to be doing in regard to anti-racist and other liberationist spiritual witness. While this intersectional book is highly practical, at its heart it feels just like sitting down with a cup of tea in the authors' presence and being drawn into an open-ended conversation that sprawls beyond the pages of this book, as one asks, what more am I being led by the Spirit to do?

Stephen W. Angell, Leatherock Professor of Quaker Studies, Earlham School of Religion, and co-editor of *Black Fire, The Oxford Handbook of Quaker Studies, The Cambridge Companion to Quakerism*

Nim Njuguna's and Jonathan Doering's *Enlarging the Tent* records a provocative and informative dialogue between two Quakers coming together to address issues of racial justice, particularly in the wake of the murder of George Floyd. In addition to providing this heart-felt and compelling dialogue, the book also includes a set of exercises for small groups of Friends to engage in discussions about what is surely a key matter for our time. I highly recommend this book as a mechanism for Friends meetings to take on the often difficult discourses of race and anti-racism work.

James W. Hood, Charles A. Dana Professor of English Emeritus, Guilford College, and editor of *Quakers and Literature*

In *Enlarging the Tent*, the reader is invited to listen in to a series of dialogues on the journey towards racial justice. These warm, enjoyable and rich conversations offer personal stories and insights to inspire, and are ideal for group study. This book will be particularly appreciated by Quakers on a similar journey to the authors, and who want to bring others along with them.

Mark Russ, Quaker theologian, blogger and author of *Quaker Shaped Christianity*

I have read works on allyship and racial justice, but none come together in quite the constructive, co-operative and conversational way as Nim and Jonathan's exchanges. They make a great basis for workshops, but also stand on their own as insights into how we might build better understanding.

Dr Helen Meads, Quaker writer and activist

The power of [their dialogue] lies in the relationship between these two kind and generous F/friends and their ability simultaneously to verbalise and demonstrate the quality of Ally-ship that we were discussing throughout the weekend.

Quaker activist, Racial Justice Conference at Bamford Quaker Community, 2022

Enlarging the Tent

Two Quakers in Conversation About
Racial Justice Dialogues and Worksheets

Enlarging the Tent

Two Quakers in Conversation About
Racial Justice Dialogues and Worksheets

Nim Njuguna and Jonathan Doering

CHRISTIAN ALTERNATIVE
BOOKS

Winchester, UK
Washington, USA

JOHN HUNT PUBLISHING

First published by Christian Alternative Books, 2023
Christian Alternative Books is an imprint of John Hunt Publishing Ltd.,
No. 3 East St., Alresford, Hampshire SO24 9EE, UK
office@jhpbooks.com
www.johnhuntpublishing.com
www.christian-alternative.com

For distributor details and how to order please visit the 'Ordering' section on our website.

ISBN: 978 1 80341 299 3
978 1 80341 300 6 (ebook)
Library of Congress Control Number: 2022914274

Design: Lapiz Digital Services

UK: Printed and bound by CPI Group (UK) Ltd, Croydon, CR0 4YY
Printed in North America by CPI GPS partners

We operate a distinctive and ethical publishing philosophy in all areas of our business, from our global network of authors to production and worldwide distribution.

Contents

In memory of George Floyd (1973–2020)

For our families and friends, and those who will come after us. This book is also dedicated to Audre Lorde, Paulo Freire, and all the people who we have never met who have still accompanied us along the way. We also gratefully acknowledge the help and support of friends, family, and of Harrow Local Quaker Meeting, and Nottinghamshire and Derbyshire Area Quaker Meeting in the production of this book.

Be aware of the spirit of God at work in the ordinary activities and experience of your daily life. Spiritual learning continues throughout life, and often in unexpected ways. There is inspiration to be found all around us, in the natural world, in the sciences and arts, in our work and friendships, in our sorrows as well as in our joys. Are you open to new light, from whatever source it may come? Do you approach new ideas with discernment?
'Advices and Queries 7', from Chapter 1 of *Quaker Faith and Practice*

[T]he master's tools will never dismantle the master's house. They may allow us temporarily to beat him at his own game, but they will never enable us to bring about genuine change.
Audre Lorde, *Sister Outsider*

To affirm that men and women are persons and as persons should be free, and yet to do nothing tangible to make this affirmation a reality, is a farce.
Paulo Freire, *Pedagogy of the Oppressed*

Preface

If you have come here to help me, you are wasting your time, but if you have come because your liberation is bound up with mine, then let us work together.

Lilla Watson

Racism is a form of violence that manifests itself within minds, souls and actions of individuals and also affects social institutions and systems. It is insidious, intelligent, affecting everyone differently. After years of social justice actions, protests, and campaigns, in the light of day and the dark of night, it works away – and so must we.

In the aftermath of the horrific murder of George Floyd by a uniformed police officer on 25 May 2020, a global outcry for social justice – largely led by the Black Lives Matter movement – ignited a racial reckoning, attracting a new generation of activists. Many were struck by the fact that it took nineteen years for two members of the racist gang who had murdered Stephen Lawrence to be brought to justice – and that a decade on, people of colour were still at daily risk of assault and murder, even at the hands of police officers tasked with protecting all citizens. Activists were willing to confront those entrenched elements of our society invested in White supremacy which still dominate the political, economic, social, and religious mainstream. This new manifestation of the movement is intent on agitating beyond incremental change-based steps to embrace transformative strategies that counter economically exploitative, psychologically oppressive and socially marginalising policies towards Black people.

Responses to Floyd's murder were manifold: political, social, emotional, artistic, religious. Just one of our responses, this

1

dialogue project between a novice and a seasoned activist is where we attempt to bring to bear our knowledge, experience and skills in order to wrestle thoughtfully and creatively with some of the issues presented by the persistent systemic racism tragically expressed in the George Floyd case, amongst many others.

When Jonathan first approached Nim, it was with the idea of a conventional interview-interviewee encounter: collaborative, but with interviewer relatively invisible and interviewee relatively exposed. What Nim suggested instead was more co-equal, involving collaboration with both bringing their thoughts and issues, working creatively with them together, through which both would hopefully grow and develop further. Rather than a synchronic snapshot conversation, this has been a longer term, diachronic project. There are no quick and easy fixes for this issue. We must commit to playing a long game.

As Quakers, our spirituality leads us to be contemplatives in action, fully engaging in the world and working for social justice informed by our core values. Entering into a meaningful dialogue for mutual benefits presupposes an equality between us, allowing for the challenging of each other's racial assumptions on our spiritual journey. Is 'Black Lives Matter' an anthem, a slogan or in reality a fact crying out for mainstreaming and implementing racial equality?

We also agreed that while dialogue is important, it is not an end in itself, as any good intentions are of limited value without corresponding on-going action. As writers we are also looking to respond creatively to new experiences and observations. Paulo Freire, whom we both admire, says that 'those who authentically commit themselves to the people must re-examine themselves constantly. This conversion is so radical as not to allow for ambivalent behaviour... Conversion to the people requires a profound rebirth. Those who undergo it must take on a new form of existence; they can no longer remain as they were'. His sentiments are echoed in those of the Diviner poet Ruth Shelton: 'Tourism brings you back home unchanged. In an encounter, you are changed forever and you never quite go back home.'

So, beginning a dialogue is an important entry-point as we move deeper in towards trying to understand one another. This is despite the discomfort and difficulties arising from talking about racism and examining our personal experiences in an extended and continuous dialogue. We were ready to question our current commitment to racial justice in action, believing social justice is more than what we do, it's about who we are, who we are becoming.

In our dialogues, we were open about our specific cultural self-awareness and orientation towards a world view that informs a Black man and a White man in a White society. We acknowledged that we were attuned differently to the subtle effects of racial bias and microaggressions in everyday interactions. We therefore brought our own experiences, values, cultures and ideas from the different communities we have grown up in, as well as the unifying Quaker spirituality in which we are immersed. Of course, we are speaking as Quakers but are not speaking officially for Quakerism in any way.

One effect of these dialogues for Jonathan has also been further reading, for instance of Audre Lorde's seminal *Sister Outsider*. In that collection of articles and other pieces, fittingly in a co-interview with fellow poet and activist Adrienne Rich, Lorde says of her time as an educationist: 'The learning process is something you can incite, literally incite, like a riot.' If the energy of new insights can spark some type of perpetual motion, not only in hearts and minds but also in actions and relationships, then we might see genuine deep-level change in the world.

There is so much to be done to resist and dismantle racism and we hope to create a space with our communities to support continuous reflection as individuals and community members to educate ourselves away from individual wrongful acts against other individuals and position ourselves to be better activists and allies for racial justice by 'speaking truth to power' to structural and systemic injustice. The way ahead is fraught on many different levels, but the possibility – and duty – of speaking truth to power is not only an action to be engaged in by those who feel brave enough. It is a necessity, sometimes unsought, that will finally be thrust upon everyone of good conscience. For, as Lorde famously cautioned: 'Your silence will not protect you.'

We humbly offer these dialogues to readers, be they Quakers, general readers with some knowledge of and interest in Quakerism, or those who wish to find out more about Quakers, as a snapshot of how two Quakers have reacted to the current situation, and their thoughts about it – both expected and unexpected – that have risen up through the dialogue process. We hope that you will find them interesting, useful, and fertile ground for developing your own thoughts and insights.

The worksheets can be used by individuals, but are intended ideally as tools to be used within a group setting and are photocopiable. We would ask that, if you use them, that you feed back to us via our publishers about their effectiveness and how they can be improved upon further.

As he sought for God's path for his life, one of the founders of Quakerism, George Fox, had to actively wrestle with various challenges, recording in his *Journal*:

> I was under great temptations sometimes... I could find none to open my condition to but the Lord alone, unto whom I cried night and day.... I saw also that there was an ocean of darkness and death, but an infinite ocean of light and love,

which flowed over the ocean of darkness. And in that also I saw the infinite love of God; and I had great openings.[1]

The 'infinite ocean of light and love' is an abiding Quaker trope, and isn't offered here as some pat and easy panacea for such a thorny and toxic problem as racism. Rather, the 'ocean of darkness and death' remains beneath the ocean of light. They continue to contend, in the world and in every human heart.

As we prepare this manuscript for publication, yet another tragedy has unfolded in New York State, where a White supremacist is standing trial for the mass murder of ten Black Americans, who he opened fire on whilst they did their shopping in a supermarket. British statistics for 2022 so far record one death of a person of colour whilst in the custody of the Metropolitan Police.[2] The case of Child Q, who was wrongly strip searched due to the incorrect suspicion of her being in possession of cannabis, has again lifted the lid on a disproportionate blanket policy of stop-and-search still applied to people of colour.[3]

Everyone must decide how they will join the contention of darkness and light.

Nim Njuguna and Jonathan Doering

London – South Yorkshire – Nakura – Nottingham, 2020–2022

1: Guilt, Blame, and How We Can Deal with Them
9 December, 2020

Jonathan's discussion point:
- Guilt – how do I/we address past actions and issues (both my own and others') constructively?
  - This pertains to my personal (mainly unconscious) privilege, and also
  - The issue of Quaker 'saints' who aren't so saintly, e.g., William Penn being revealed to have owned enslaved people.

Nim's discussion point:
- In what ways am I advancing the cause of social and racial justice, informed by Quaker values within my sphere of influence?

Personal Work First

Jonathan Doering: Maybe we just need to take the plunge and start talking through these topics. I mean, if you were looking to have a conversation about an issue, using this approach, how would you frame it, how would you normally start off?

Nim Njuguna: I think… for me it's caught up in that self-reflection. The quality of my contribution to my Meeting is in direct proportion to my work in the Spirit. That relates to the quality of my spirituality, which of course leads me to include every human being… if I haven't done private work to be ready to be able to progress the social justice agenda, informed by Quaker values in my sphere of influence, I *cannot* contribute to my Quaker Meeting or my wider community. Sometimes my contribution to the Meeting is from an ego-position, from what we theologically call 'the flesh', so for me it is about: how do I get myself ready to contribute to my Meeting, and how do I get my Meeting to get ready to contribute to the World, because if we aren't practising what we're preaching, we won't be very effective [*he laughs*].

Forgiveness and Dialogue

NN: The next thing is what we've both alluded to in our discussion points, which is mind-set. What kind of mind-set is required in order to make this journey that has both positive and negative challenges, which are sometimes guilt inducing? For me, that means forgiving myself and others. If I can forgive myself and others, then I'm in the right frame of mind. When I'm doing my research about race and other emotive, difficult issues, if I can practise forgiveness, then I'm in the right frame of mind. So, when we come to look at the past, whether we call it reparation or delayed justice, again it's that mind-set, because for me when I'm able to forgive myself and others, I can move to interdependence. It's not a *debate*: it's a *dialogue*. It's not about winning, about what they did in the past, who was right, who was wrong.... This is what happened in the past, now what do we do? That's a mind-set of redeeming the past, so we extract what is important for today's redemption, then go forward. All those people holding on to anger and resentment and unforgiveness, they're not going to take us anywhere, in practical terms.

Writing academic papers, oh yes, you can write academic papers and show all of your arguments historically, sociologically, economically, but here we're talking about advancing the cause of social justice in order to move from othering to belonging. Now it's the 'how', which I think you're much more experienced with. I prepare my lessons and I go and teach (!). You interview people, and you know how to frame all of this... given that framework, I return the question to you: how would *you* work with it? How would *you* approach it?

JD: That's a good question.... I need to get this clear in my mind, because up till now my experience of interviewing has been traditional in the sense that I've approached somebody, because they're interesting to me, they're a writer, academic or whatever, we've agreed to have an interview. Then I've read about issues, read their work. I've thought up some questions. We have a conversation, where I'm asking questions and some of them I've sent on ahead and the interviewee has thought about them, whilst others arise naturally in the course of the conversation, but it's been weighted towards the interviewee. So I'm actively listening.... Of course, I will sometimes chip comments in, but my main contribution is hopefully well-crafted, thoughtful questions which will assist and facilitate the interviewee in opening up whatever the topic is that we're discussing. What I think we've agreed to do here is more like a co-interview.

Otherness and Belonging

NN: Yes, it's more of a dialogue, a conversation. We're bridging between these two points.... We have been bequeathed this otherness through our socialisation. You will go through this life as a White person, I'll go through this life as a Black person. That is plus social identities, spiritual identities, political identities, economic identities... whatever else we attach to that. What we have in common first of all is a desire to bridge the gap between otherness and belonging. And that belonging is firstly a belonging to the human race. With the environmental catastrophe, you won't survive, whether you're White or Black, man or woman, short or tall. There's that shared humanity.

Secondly, I don't know whether we discussed this before, but my approach is: everybody is like everybody else. So, you and I have so much in common that allows us to have an authentic discussion. However, some people are like certain other people, but not like others! Which means you and I belong to two different realities, if you like. On the one hand we share things in common; on the other hand, you belong to one tribe, I belong to another.

Thirdly, whether you're from one tribe or another, we're unique individuals. There's no way you can treat me as *just* a Black person, there's no way I can treat you as *just* a White person. You are *this* White person and I am *this* Black person. And this White person and this Black person happen to be Quakers who have been spiritually shaped and *that*, our common humanity, gives us the courage to proceed. Our 'unique uniqueness' as individuals and as Quakers gives us the spiritual nurture to proceed. However, we also know that this middle group where you belong to some people and I belong to others... these are in the world, our society, our Quaker Meetings, but they're not necessarily having this dialogue we are having. They are not reading the books that we've been reading. They are not necessarily motivated to do this. We are engaging in this to take it back to them, and when we take it back to them, we are offering 'common humanity', as Quakers. Therefore, let us start with something positive. Sometimes when we talk about the past, we talk as if there were not Quakers. There were Quakers who happened to own slaves, and there were Quakers who did not own slaves, so in terms of 'unique individuals', that's one example of where we have multiple identities. With these multiple identities, why do we only zoom in on one that is negative? It might be very significant and we need to talk about it, not forgetting that the person, based on uniqueness, has multiple identities. You're a husband, a father, a teacher, a writer, a community development worker... you've got all these things. So for me, we have a pretty good starting point, where we give each other psychological permission, and for me that *psychological permission* opens up the dialogue. It's about finding common understanding, common ground. And we have three things on our side: our common humanity, our common Quakerism, and our unique individuality.

Of course, that common humanity is why a Black person can sometimes give blood to a White person or donate a liver. We share things in common. Our common Quakerism, our spirituality that is informed by a particular experience. Our unique individual identities are informed by our individual experiences. Not every White, male Quaker has been to Kenya for instance, and met the kind of people you've met. Not every Quaker is married to a vicar like you are! [*They laugh.*] All these unique individual aspects give us a particular means of engagement. Unless you get to know the purpose, you end up saying, 'Oh, a White person, Black person, woman...' you don't *know* the person unless you have a unique encounter which is a kind of belonging. Where, and how, do we belong?

Sharing Lived Experiences

JD: I agree with that. At this point I'll acknowledge that this is moving into different territory for me. Obviously in lots of contexts I have talked and do talk about myself, but in the context of interviewing I haven't been there to reveal so much of myself but rather to work with someone else in discovering things about their experience or what they've got to say on a particular issue. This will be different for me in that there's going to have to be some revelation at certain points of things that I've done and my own experience and my feelings about that as well, which ordinarily wouldn't feature. But as you say, this isn't an interview so much, it's a *co*-interview. It's different.

NN: This is where I say we're giving each other the psychological permission to not get it *right*. There's no tick box here, because we're sharing from our own lived experience, whether it's from memory, the here and now, or imagination. This is not marked work, this is two individuals who have embarked on a journey, both of self-discovery and mutuality in order to be ready to facilitate other people at some point. I think it would be a good idea, Jonathan, what you said originally, to just go down the list of our discussion points. You do your number one, I do my number one. We reach a conclusion at some point, however long that takes.

JD: That sounds like a way forward. Are you suggesting then over the coming weeks we work down these two lists of questions that we've got, discussing them to our mutual satisfaction?

NN: Yes, because, I think the notes you've taken, what we're taping, we've got enough background.

JD: Alright. Would you like to go with your first point, or would you prefer for me to kick off?

NN: If you're alright to go with your first point, that'll be fine.

White Fragility and Guilt: Resistance to Revisionism

JD: Right. Guilt – how do I/we address past actions and issues (both my own and others') constructively? I'm thinking here about my personal (mainly unconscious) privilege, also the issue of Quaker 'saints' who aren't so saintly, e.g., William Penn being revealed to have owned enslaved people. I know we've talked about this, but I think it is still [he sighs] for me as a White middle-class man, it's always there, I think, this issue of guilt. How do I, and how do we, and 'we' meaning you and me, but also in a wider sense, for our purposes Meetings and our friends in our Quaker Meetings, address past actions and issues? Those 'actions and issues' could be my own actions and issues, but also others', making whatever we do to address it constructive and meaningful, rather than just breast-beating or denial or avoidance.

That for me at the moment splits into two major branches. It relates to my own personal and probably mostly unconscious privilege and the fact that, living as a White middle-class man in Britain at the moment I'm mainly shielded from the worst effects of climate change.

Having been to Kenya, having seen the extreme poverty there, my wife and I now try to limit ourselves to one cup of coffee a day rather than two or three. I mean we might have the second cup sometimes, but we don't have more than two cups of coffee a day [*he laughs*] which I know is a very small thing but.... I woke up to the fact that the vast majority of Kenyans who we met don't ever drink coffee. It's farmed there as a cash crop and most of them either can't afford it or there's absolutely no good reason for them to purchase it, even if they could eke out the money to do that. My wife and I felt rather ashamed about that. I mean if we wanted to, we could drink a lot of coffee every day and it wouldn't set us back financially. That's obviously a symptom of a wider global economic issue.

Then the second branch is, and this links with the document that I sent to you that my friend at Barnsley Meeting has put together, about the issues of Quaker 'saints', who aren't so saintly, like William Penn. I have to say it's all come up rather suddenly, that Penn was a person who owned enslaved people, but the truth is, and I'm not trying to point the finger at anyone, if that had been generally on the record, I would have been aware of it... I'm not saying I'm an expert on Penn, but I've read a bit about him. It's sitting there on the record, but we haven't really talked about that, haven't really seized that nettle. It hasn't really been present in discussions around Penn up to this point.

It's great that the Black Lives Matter movement, if I can use that as shorthand, has woken us up more to a whole range of issues and this is one of them. It's all very well supporting removing certain statues in public places of slave owners, which personally I think is a good thing. There does need to be a discussion around it, what you do with that statue, whether it's destroyed or put out of sight entirely or used as part of an ongoing discussion about these issues. As a teacher, it strikes me that exhibiting and discussing these statues differently is one constructive response.

It's all very well supporting all of that, but we Quakers have got to look to our own house, and there is William Penn's name on a room in Friends House; is that appropriate?[1] It was quite interesting, we discussed this a couple of weeks ago, and one Friend at Meeting said, 'I think I have an issue with *any* names being put on *any* rooms in Friends House. Should we be doing that at all?' But of course, that's a far wider question than what we're dealing with here. It's so important, and my friend has acknowledged in their document on Penn that we've got to own our own history. Our history is ourselves, so it's not about denying it, or trying to excise it completely, but it's about how you work with it, in an honest and beneficial way. Maybe this is the moment for me to stop talking and give you a chance to respond.

Economic Privilege

NN: Yes... with guilt, there are two things. I also live a very privileged life in Kenya. I have people who work for me. They are paid better than other people doing the same work. They get a house; they get a piece of land to grow their own food. Some relatives think I am totally wrong! I have a very good friend, she was an ambassador, and she couldn't understand why I was giving them a job description: 'Nim, you're sending out the wrong signals. Use your power, dominate them!' So for me, the whole thing about guilt-feelings.... I separate the two things, there is guilt and guilt-feelings. It is easy to deal with guilt-feelings, as they come and go. It might be something I do. I might sometimes feel guilty about eating too much.... I have also had to come to terms with the fact that I was an only child, my parents went to school in the Twenties, they happened to be a doctor and a midwife. Therefore, they accrued some land. It's how I assuage my guilt by giving back something, acknowledging I'm not going to give everything away so that I'm left destitute. I will help no one if I end up in that condition.

Equally, I will help no one if I'm immobilised by being guilt-ridden. I came to terms with my guilt and my guilt-feelings in order to be able to not focus on myself. What I'm talking about now, it's what I feel about 'servant leadership'. I serve, from a leadership position, because I have the resources. My employees don't have my kind of education; they didn't go to university like me. They don't own land. They don't do the kinds of jobs we do, some of them don't have a bank account. That's their reality, and this is my reality. I cannot deny the guilt, but I assuage my guilt by taking these steps. Sometimes I'm overwhelmed by the need. I know I can't meet it all, and that's when the guilt-feelings start to come in. The original guilt is gone [*he chuckles*] but guilt-feelings – 'Oh God, I wish I could help this one and the other one....' – that will always be there. But that's your guilt on the basis of *being*, not what you have *done*.

The Need to Be Proactive

NN: Because you haven't kept slaves, you haven't trafficked anyone, yours is a guilt of being.

JD: Yes, in the main... I just have to add the rider that, like lots of other people in developed countries, I benefit from the fact that people in the developing world are not as enfranchised as I am and therefore many – not all, but many – work for very low wages to produce clothing, food and other goods that people like me take for granted a lot of the time. But I suppose that's more *being* rather than *doing*, certainly not actively seeking to do anything inappropriate or wrong. But when does inaction become complicity?

This raises the point that's come into currency of late, this idea that it's one thing to not be racist, but that's rather passive and apathetic. If you're going to be anti-racist, that means you've got to be *active*, actively saying and doing things as well, which is a kind of call to action, I think – particularly to White people.

It's fresh in my head today because I've been looking at a chart that my friend has included in the Quaker history document that I mentioned before, that's been put together by an Asian academic at Sheffield University. He talks about these four positions that White people can adopt in terms of race relations and racism. There's White Supremacy on the one extreme, then White Indifference, moving across to White Awareness, and finally White Allyship. There are descriptions of responses and attitudes and so on under each of those headings, and that whole point... if someone says, 'I'm not a racist,' what does that really *mean*? Truly, people are either indifferent or they're aware, which is somewhat better. But we're talking ideally about allyship, and how do you *wake up*, how do you take practical, meaningful steps? It's one thing to say it, but that's not really enough, you've got to do something, I think. It's like Jesus of Nazareth saying in the Bible, 'Those who are not for me are against me.' It's the same thing. This strikes across everything, across issues of class inequality, racial inequality, sexual inequality, gender inequality. You can't just say, 'I don't agree with that inequality.' That means that you have to do something about it, which doesn't *necessarily* mean standing on the barricades. [*He laughs.*] But it does mean that you've got to try to take practical steps in your own life that *mean something*.

NN: I don't know whether you read my article on 'The Journey' in the *Quarterly*? I have eight categories of Allyship there.[2]

Looking at Issues with New Eyes
NN: It's about being on the journey. I'm writing there about journeying with this person. It's very interesting, it's like us. I was saying to him, we are equally privileged in different ways, and I'm taking him to my side of the rails, so to speak. It would be helpful if you could get a copy. Now for me, there are two

things we've said. Also, you've intimated about your Meeting. Unless and until we are initiated to read a text and say, 'Where are Black people in this text? Where are disabled people in this text? Where are women? Where are Muslims? Where are LGBTQ people?' If you have not been initiated, you will read about all the Quaker Greats, and you'll miss out certain nuances, because you haven't been *adjusted* to read like that. This is part of what you're doing and part of what you're doing in your Meeting – being adjusted and initiated to be able to look at the same reality differently.

Finding a Starting Point on the Continuum

NN: Why I take some issue with the four positions... I don't discard them, they're absolutely very helpful. But I start with a continuum that runs from novice to expert and everything else in between, developing a greater sense of nuance. My question is, when did you become a novice? When did you agree to look at these issues with an open mind? The next question is, what *kind* of novice are you? Is it a novice who wants to listen and learn? Because what you're telling me is an alternative history. I've never been taught this; I've never heard this before. How do I know it is true? But you have said you are coming onto the continuum, because it will end up with you being an expert – again I'm using these words very loosely... This is why I say we need to give each other the permission to get it wrong. As a novice in this dialogue, we don't have to get it right. We are on this continuum. We've started. We've done our homework, and this is something we need to do.

Now, *some* White people, some who are sexist and homophobic and all that, they have not stepped onto the continuum. They haven't said, 'I'm going to shut up and learn.' What I have been told may be true, but as Jesus said about the coin, 'Give to Caesar what belongs to Caesar, give to God what belongs to God.' There are two sides to every story. If somebody does not accept that there are two sides to every story [*he laughs*] it's very difficult to get them to be a novice, on this issue of race, or the whole notion of intersectionality, because the books they've read, the experiences they've had, the meaning-making, has excluded the other side of the coin.

You saw the other side of the coin and said, 'One cup of coffee,' because you've seen the other side. Without the other side, oh, coffee all the time! [*He chuckles.*] My story is from one side. There are people who will not agree to be initiated and therefore are not on the journey, beginning as novices on this continuum. I had another article a while ago in the *Friend*, where I talked about an 'across-the-road mate'. I also had a bed mate, a roommate, a house mate, next-door mate....

JD: That sounds very useful, nuancing different experiences of one's consciousness being raised.

NN: That article grew out of me asking, 'What do I do with this White person who is not ready, who denies all this?' Then the question comes, 'Can I have a dialogue, not necessarily on the race issue?' Because remember I'm being driven by the notion of common humanity. There is no way that I'm going to negate this person's common humanity. The caveat for that is what Jesus said – as far as it is possible, be at peace with every person. *As far as it is possible.* There is a cut-off point to accommodating another person. But they don't become a non-person, because I would never make them a non-person.

I go back to the biblical story of the young man who came to Jesus and asked, 'What should I do to inherit the Kingdom of God?' Jesus tells him, 'Sell everything and give to the poor.' The young man refused; he turned and went away. Jesus was sad but he still loved him. I cannot deny my sadness when there have been people who I have liked yet known that they have said racist things. So there is a cut-off point. It's not a rejection. This is where in some families during Christmas dinner you know Uncle Peter and Auntie June will be kept at separate ends of the table. That's the only way we're going to have a good Christmas dinner, if they're sitting separately! So there are some people in our Meetings whose credentials, where race relations are concerned, are dodgy.

I believe we have multiple identities; therefore I look for one identity that I can work with. Maybe this person is a stamp collector – yeah, a racist stamp collector! Let's talk about stamps, let's not talk about race. But in order to be there you have to have worked through this continuum. You can't do it as a novice. If we set our five points on the continuum, and the fifth one is where you become an expert, I'm talking about someone who has achieved the state of forgiving themselves and others. They're not necessarily an expert in an academic sense. They're comfortable in their own skin, their own humanity, their skeleton and all. *That* for me is the expert bit. You're not hiding: warts and all, it's there. I have worked through the continuum. It's like when I would ask somebody, 'When did you become anti-racist? When did you become anti-sexist? When did you become pro-gay?' They might say, 'I don't know – I was just born that way,' there are people who seem to find it much easier to do than others. You show them the continuum, and they jump there immediately. Within a very short time they've jumped from being a novice to the second stage. Others take a long, long time. They resist, they have to be convinced.

Small Surprises

NN: There are massive ironies around all of this. One person who stood up in the House of Commons and defended Kenyans mistreated by the British government was Enoch Powell! Nobody else. In Hansard, he was quoted as standing up and challenging that. In that identity you can't say, 'Oh, I'll never quote Enoch Powell because of what he did later on.' He also did that, which was something good. Historically *that* part was *right*.[3] He could be horribly wrong in many other ways, but that part was right. It's about finding common ground with this person who is racist. Otherwise, are we going to say we'll never talk?

Initial Practical Steps

NN: Do we have time to talk through my Number 1?

JD: If you'd like to do that, that would be good, then we've done both number ones. That's a good idea.

NN: For me, if I come back to my Number 1, it was my reflection. I have written this more than once, because it is very powerful for me. It's really asking myself, in what ways am I advancing the cause of social and racial justice, informed by Quaker values within my sphere of influence? Because if I'm not advancing the cause of social and racial justice, what am I doing?

If I'm asked, 'In the last year, in the last month, in the last week, what have you done?' is it a blame culture? I cannot advance the cause of social and racial justice with blame, apportioning blame, with unforgiveness. I cannot advance that without a spirituality that tells me that I live in a world that is not complete, because no human being is complete in themselves. Equally I know in order to advance the cause of social and racial justice, I have to find like-minded people, fellow-travellers. People who believe the world is not the way it could be, but we don't just sit back and blame other people – there are things we can be doing within our sphere of influence. We start where we are. That is why I was saying in terms of Kenyan people, I can give them part of my land, I can pay them their wages, I can give them a house to live in. In the past I've educated some of their children. *That's* what I'm doing in order to be advancing with them.

In my Meeting there are things I can do. I started a film club. Most of the films we've seen, the members would *never* have seen. [*He chuckles.*] World films. Now they expect to watch

World Cinema. 'It's amazing to me, y'know? That's what they do in Arabic countries?' They're on the continuum. Like you say – one cup of coffee. They're talking about Arabic films and that's a step, they weren't talking about them yesterday. I wanted it to be about Quaker-related themes. Whether it's writing in a Quaker journal or an American theological journal, it's about thinking as a Quaker: my sphere of influence, my home, my Local Meeting, my Yearly Meeting, Woodbrooke, Friends House... what kind of influence can one have? But I can't do that without the mind-set that says, 'I cannot fight for social and racial justice while at the same time merely zooming in on injustices, whether that's past injustices, present injustices, I must do something about them.'

NN: That can take various forms.... Part of my sphere of influence in the past was writing to Profumo.[4] Writing to Helen Suzman. She was the only liberal White South African MP.[5] My sphere of influence included writing to Bishop Casey when he had fathered a child.[6] Each one of them wrote back. That's a sphere of influence. Profumo said, 'Thank you, it's good to hear from a stranger recognising my other work, other than getting hammered.' Within my sphere of influence, I can do something immediate, ameliorating people's conditions, some of it is just letter writing, article writing.

JD: At this stage I should respond now, I think.

All of that sounds very positive, very deep, very logical, very integrated. What was at the back of my mind is that you were talking about setting up a film club, then also, in a slightly different way, writing letters, and writing articles which are things I do. Sometimes the challenge comes, and you've got to seize the nettle, you've got to do something that you're going to find challenging, difficult, perhaps even dangerous or unpleasant, and sometimes this kind of change calls for that. But also, a lot of it is about finding things that you love to do anyway, and if you can somehow interweave what you like, what you enjoy doing, what you love doing, with what needs to be done, then it will be that bit easier to do it. You know that advice in Colossians 3.23: 'Whatever you do, do it with all of your heart.' That's very wise. Years ago, when I'd just started attending Quaker Meeting, a Young Quaker, who'd been a Quaker all of his life, and was an activist, talked about that, about how the trick was, if you could find things that people *wanted* to do, *enjoyed* doing, then of course they would do them more. Someone could argue that you might view that as a selfish aspect to good works. Well, yes and no, because if we enjoy whatever we do, of course we'll do more of it, we'll enjoy doing that, and that becomes a virtuous circle. I don't want to suggest that that's all of it, but it's important. I think that also then connects with this idea of looking for common ground with people, because it's true, I mean we all know people who are prejudiced in different ways. I know that I do have prejudice myself, which I have to deal with.

It's echoing through my head what you said that this is all really about making peace with yourself, and admitting or acknowledging that we're all a mixture of light and dark, I'm a mixture of light and dark, and not projecting the dark bits onto other people, demonising them, and making myself feel so much better by comparison [*they chuckle*].

NN: Yes.

JD: I'm a mix. They're a mix. I've got to accept that about myself, then I can accept it about them. Without saying, 'This is okay, the dark bits are okay and therefore we tolerate or even celebrate them.' We've got to say what is acceptable or not in ourselves and over time we've got to work with others to hopefully help them to be able to do that with themselves. But that's a work of a long time. It's evolutionary, not revolutionary!

NN: It is, Jonathan, and again we mentioned very early on, I can remember mentioning, a third of the people are people like us, a third need persuasion, that is the whole *conscientization* of

Freire, and we need to work on their consciousness, and the last third, they don't want to be. They're the young rich ruler who doesn't accept what Jesus said. One thing I haven't mentioned, but whilst you were speaking it came to mind. About four years ago, I went through eighteen months of the Dark Night of the Soul. A horrible eighteen months. I was still accompanying people with spiritual direction, I was still doing things, but it was where for eighteen months there was a cloud, a dry experience. Then I woke up one morning and it was all gone, and I think the poems I wrote during that time depict that. So that's another thing that we go through where our own growth, development, questioning, 'Dark Night', whatever you want to call it, I think it's a moment of adjusting.

JD: And it's not always comfortable, I suppose there has to be discomfort as well.

2: Threat = Opportunity? Actions and Reactions
16 December, 2020

Jonathan's discussion point:
- How can we effectively act on awareness, even when there are people who will react against this work?

Nim's discussion point:
- Why is diversity by some within our Quaker community seen as a threat rather than an opportunity, and what can we do about that?

The Relevance of Past to Present
We began by discussing an article by Jonathan about the George Floyd Case and the Black Lives Matter Movement. Nim was preparing a training session for the Woodbrooke Quaker Study Centre, plus research on Bayard Rustin (a veteran Black American civil rights and LGBTQ activist) and a history project about colonialism in Kenya....

NN: I think most of the things that I'm currently working on, for me, are about the question, what's the *relevance* of the past to the present? The past happened, we can read it from the present in order to extract useful meaning, but equally to correct the record, also to inform the future. So for me when I'm dealing with Bayard Rustin, *why* is he relevant? At a very basic level, it's a celebration of a life well-lived in the public arena, advancing the cause of social, racial and environmental justice. You're saying, here is a story that hasn't been told in a particular way, and if it is told in a particular way for these times.... We do the same thing with our Quaker continuing revelation. Then turning to the Bible, this book that was written thousands of years ago: why is it relevant today? Those are the things that have been going on in my mind, whether we are talking about Penn, Bayard, the past, its relevance for today.

JD: Interesting.

NN: Number Twos...

Effectively Acting on Awareness

NN: I was looking at them and they seem very similar. They dovetail somewhere, I think. Do you want to go first?

JD: Okay, 'How can we effectively act on awareness? Even when there are people who will react against this work?' I'm talking about the challenge for *me*, it's one thing I'm very much into developing my knowledge, understanding, awareness, and thought processes. But ultimately, you've got that question, what are you going to *do* about it? It comes down to that challenge. When I first became a Quaker, there was that period of great excitement, when I first discovered Quaker worship and so on. It was wonderful. I felt like all these wonderful insights were coming to me, and I was sitting there in Meeting one day and this voice in my head asked, 'What are you going to *do* about it now? Now that you've found this wonderful worship and this wonderful religious way of life.' [*He laughs.*] But in fact, that's the same for every single aspect of my life. That's why I've written this question. What can I do and what ought I to do? Also knowing that there will be people who will react against it, and people who will be quite apathetic, but also the people who may have a vested interest in me not doing anything very much about it, or not bothering them with it.... I don't know if this is entirely relevant, but if it's alright, I can bring in my experience in community development at this stage.

NN: Sure, go ahead.

JD: In this role my colleague and I carry out research and support initiatives aimed at fostering racial equality and integration. As part of that remit, we've looked into the provision of English for Speakers of Other Languages (ESOL) in our area, as well as the experience of BAME residents in seeking, securing and holding work. I don't want to be unfair to anyone, because overall I have felt well-supported, and I've felt people have been very open to what we are trying to do. That said, a recent project that we worked on, which we found really interesting and hopefully it'll do some good, was to examine the experience of BAME people in terms of employment in our area. Experiences when looking for work, when they've got work, whether they've been able to get work, is it the kind of work that they would wish to have, that they're qualified for or do they just have to take what comes along?

Muted and Hostile Responses

JD: The general mood music has been positive, but I have to say, there have been people in the area who, on paper I would have expected to have been more supportive of it, but in fact they've been quite muted. Y'know, maybe I'm being a bit paranoid, but I don't think I am. [*He chuckles.*] It seems that there have been certain people who would prefer for us not to go there, really. Not lift the lid on that particular can of worms.

That said, there have been certain employers who've been very supportive, who were very quick to respond and gave us detailed, positive information... the vast majority of those who responded, you might describe as model employers. They were doing the right thing or trying very hard. There were a couple who came back, you know, and their employment rates were actually really rather low, and in one case [*he chuckles*] they had absolutely no interest in receiving any training or any other input, but they still engaged in the process. But that was *one* employer out of maybe twelve or fifteen who came back to us.

You know, now and again you get open hostility, but more often it's a very good way of killing off what someone wants to do by being very quiet, muted and polite, and not responding. It's like a wet blanket dropping over something. That can kill things off very effectively. I suppose that kind of links in with discernment. I'm not suggesting that Quaker discernment is necessarily a wet blanket! What I'm going on to say is, obviously when we're seized with enthusiasm and a little bit of fire as Quakers, specifically, of course it's much better if we then take half a step back and take a breath and think about precisely what we're proposing to do, why we feel led to do it, and how we're going to do it, and discuss that with other Quakers. So that discernment process, that's very valuable and important....

NN: Yes, it is.

JD: Whilst also saying, maybe not with every last single enthusiasm that comes along, but certainly with a lot of the issues and the events, factors, people and groups that we feel inspired to engage with, we must also be careful not to lose the momentum as well, I suppose.

Quaker Business Method and the 'Overseer' Term

JD: That's quite a ramble, but actually it comes back to Quakers specifically, there's a challenge there, isn't there? I think at one time or another all Quakers have felt frustrated with the discernment process, if it's led to a relatively long time lag between their sense of being inspired and something happening, although experientially I would say overall it's always been for the best to reflect and talk things over prayerfully and in a reflective, thoughtful way.

This seems to link in with the whole national debate around the use of the term 'overseer'. We discussed this at my local Meeting quite extensively when that started to come through in the letters pages of *The Friend*. It certainly spoke to me when I read it. I felt strongly that we ought to be discussing it and seeing what we thought, and we had several really good and positive discussions about it at Business Meeting. I have to say broadly there were two sides to the argument. It wasn't that everyone automatically said, 'Absolutely, we've got to think about this term, and we've got to talk about changing it.' There were quite a few people who agreed, but there were other people who said, 'We're aware that this particular term is problematic, but there are issues....' Someone was concerned that we didn't then spiral into changing all of our language. Other people made the point that in our context it was being sued supportively.

Anyway, the concern was passed up to Meeting for Sufferings by several Area Meetings, which I was personally pleased about. I understand that they had a really positive discussion. There were moments when we were talking about it as a local meeting where I was aware that potentially I could feel a bit frustrated, and I know that we're still on that road, it's still being discussed, it's still being worked on, but it does now feel like there's some positive movement on it. We've just been tiny cogs in all of that, which is fine. Why I've brought the story in is there were moments where I was on the edge of feeling a bit frustrated: 'Oh, gosh, are we *ever* going to agree to inch forward on it?' But then it *did* come through. It moved up through the chain, as it were, through the system so that's good....

The next thing that comes up in my head is that you have to trust the system, as long as the format and the system and the framework are ones that you understand, and you accept and believe in. Even if they're not perfect, because they won't be, overall, you accept them. That for me is a success story for the Quaker Business Method because ultimately, we haven't reached an end point with that issue yet, but in terms of that little stage of the story, that has developed positively. It just took a bit longer. Ideally, if I could press a button and set it to a particular time frame.... At the time I might have preferred it to happen a bit faster, but as I talk to you, I think maybe one or two more people ended up coming along with us and coming round to that particular viewpoint. That's with the caveat that it's not about me or any other individual particularly persuading other people of things, it's about an issue and a particular view or perspective that is legitimate and beneficial gaining the traction that it deserves. And sometimes a particular issue may not gain traction at a certain point because it isn't the right time. In the long run I think that part of the story is a little success story because that did happen and it did take *time*. I suppose all of this is... going to take time. But it's important if we're maintaining momentum.

Alongside that there is that issue of people who may react against the work, and that could be with open hostility. I mean, I remember some of the letters in *The Friend* around the use of that term 'overseer', people quoting the fact that it's just a transliteration of the Greek for 'bishop', which would be someone who provided pastoral oversight. Of course other people are entitled to their view of a situation, but personally when I read that, I felt a little that in those circumstances that felt a little like not engaging with and discussing with an understanding of language. If you're going to have positive forward movement... not necessarily with everyone saying, 'We're all going to adopt one particular perspective,' but you've got to have a little porosity, even if you're saying, 'Well, my understanding is this, and I can see yours is different.' That extra porosity allows our understandings to potentially bleed across to each other. That brings me back to that Quakerly practice of sometimes kicking the can down the road, which can be the result of very prolix, drawn-out discernment and decision-making processes. That's my question really, how do we work positively with that? Are there particular techniques that we could or should come up with? Or is it more just about 'naming the game'? Being aware of that situation and if we're conscious of it, maybe that will allow us to move through it. I'll be quiet now!

Three Key Responses
NN: As you were talking, the things that were going through my mind were: a) again, something we've talked about before,

which is the way I categorize things; a third of the people will understand, comprehend, will be pro-, and therefore these are fellow travellers, because if I have what I believe is a good, legitimate view, it isn't only given to *me* exclusively, it is shared with other people, which is the whole concept of the *invention*, whatever invention, whether it was an American, a German was doing it, when you look at things that were invented, the light bulb... other people were *doing* it... the *cinema* – other people, a year later... other people would have developed it, so this is.... I believe we are given visions, and it's about finding kindred spirits who are *ready-made*. We don't *make* them, we don't *persuade* them, they are *already there*. Some of them are even ahead of us. So that is the one-third that for me gives me a lot of courage and motivation.

Then you find another one-third, they are not sure and some of them don't easily take to things without analysing, thinking through. If it's a strange concept, they have to mull it over. But they are positive people, they are seekers, they want to find truth, they want to know – this new thing doesn't sound quite right, but I'm willing to spend time thinking about it, praying about it, analysing it.

Then of course you always have the third who oppose. Or as you say, they can even kill it with kindness, they don't have to be actively opposing it. Actively opposing, killing with kindness, sitting on the fence... and some of them are the ones, given the issues, where we can't be spending a lot of time, because if you put new wine into old wine skins, the wine skins won't hold it! It's a waste of time to put new wine in old wine skins. But we are also peace makers, and again as Jesus said, as far as it is possible be at peace with everybody, we must try to be. As far as it is *possible*. So there are people, I'm not going to interact with them, because as far as it is possible, I can't make peace with them. Equally, there are three stages when we look at this, people in organisations like ours, as Quakers, with that vestige of awareness, which has to do with hearts and minds. Have you been captured by the vision? In your heart? In your mind? Do you then derive a purpose from that vision, that the purpose now which is informed by my values and beliefs, where I inject my feeling and passion, because this is what I'm now aware that I should do? Here's a simple, personal story. Last December, I went through a period, thinking that if I treated my mind, soul and spirit the way I treat my body, I'd be a wreck! [*Both laugh.*] I really thought through that and on 14 December when I went to bed, I decided I would start treating my body differently. A year later, I have lost a stone and a half. Eight of the ten medications for diabetes that I was taking, have been taken out....

JD: Congratulations, that's good.

Finding Our Vision

NN: The reason I'm saying it is that there came a time it had to be my *heart purpose*, my *vision*, finally [*he chuckles*] and I *had* to do it. And that has become a vision thing. So, before this meeting I was at the gym. You start a new way of *reading* the same reality. The reality is the same, the *meaning* you derive from that reality is different. The meaning I used to derive from the food I used to eat, the amount I used to eat, all that, is different.... My life hasn't changed so dramatically, it's just the meanings that attach to things.

I see the problem with us Quakers is sometimes people have marginal awareness but want to take maximum action, but it can't happen – you firstly have to bed in the awareness. Because that awareness then brings you to what you could call capacity building. Now, that capacity building is what I'm saying – again, sorry to be using myself as a case study here.... You then begin a totally different behaviour and norms and practices. You start developing a new skill base. You start communicating differently, you start measuring an outcome, but that only comes because you've got this awareness to try and inject norms and behaviours, for example, anti-racism into some of our Meetings that haven't gone through the awareness stage. They're still rejecting ideas, concepts. This brings us to my question, I think: Why is diversity seen by some within our Quaker community as a threat rather than an opportunity, and what can we do about that?

I don't know if I've told you this. In one Quaker Meeting they had a Black Lives Matter flag. Some horrible person came and burned it. I understand that the Friend in Residence was being blamed by some others who were saying, 'We're for the environment, we're not for Black Lives Matter,' and you think, 'Yes....' [*Sighs.*] There is no hierarchy, they don't understand that, they don't understand that it is not one against the other. When we crystallise so quickly in terms of expected behaviour and norms without having a proper awareness, I think we do a disservice, because people haven't bought into the story.

It's as if some Friends who sit with us in our Meeting have always voted one political party. They've always voted that way! What is going to shift them to vote differently? Because they *don't* look at the issues. They don't build their awareness about these issues, they just say, 'I'm a Conservative, I am Green, I am...' and that becomes a default position that they take everywhere. Because then we come to the third stage which is about structures, awareness that leads to behaviour, norms and then the structures that will support and carry that. That's where systemic racism, the systems and policies... unless they change, all that good work of awareness and capacity building will falter. That's where strategies come in.... So, what *are* the strategies? We have to rewrite our staff books, our manuals, our strategic plans, our five-year plans. It might mean that we need to bring in people externally because we don't have the capacity to write it this way, especially with race issues.... It's as if you're taking an English manual and you're writing it in French, and you want someone with no French to try to write it. You can't!

Your O-Level French will not help you to write this. So, with policy change, budgets, who decides why *this* is a budget item? Why is this other issue *not* a budget item?

When you reach that, it's where in some Meetings they don't yet have the capacity to link things, to say to young people, 'If you are just shopping and wearing it once and throwing it away and buying another one, because it is cheap and you can afford to, do you know *where* it comes from? Do you know *who* is making it? Do you know *how much* they are being paid?'

I visited an Indian guy in Kenya. He was only making wrappers for coffee tins, and he was telling me, 'I'm paid more for my wrapper around this coffee tin than coffee workers are paid for the amount of coffee they produce to go into this tin, which will then be sold for five, ten times more.' Until people can make those links, that we've got to take care of each other and the environment, we won't have progress.

Take whales. You could say, 'They live in the water!' – 'Ye-es, they live in the water!' For me, it's those things, when do we get this awareness, when does this capacity building come, when the norms and the people change and they see it as the normal thing, therefore when we come to talk about rewriting our Red Book [*Quaker Faith and Practice*] and doing other things, you are awash with awareness, but I'm sure there may be people writing the Red Book without saying to themselves, 'I must become a more encompassing person.' That is what we all need to try to be: encompassing.

JD: This is all really interesting and very important. When you were talking about things like marginal awareness and how that can't support maximum action, and building capacity through building awareness and so on, that prompted me to wonder, is there a particular approach? In the event that a group of people were sitting down to talk about these things, is it a good idea for us to discuss potential techniques or materials or things like that…. [*He laughs.*] I'm not necessarily suggesting that we ideastorm detailed materials here and now, but is it worth us asking how can we avoid some of those pitfalls and introduce beneficial mind-sets to support that kind of constructive dialogue for groups of people?

Now Is a Kairos Moment

NN: Two or three things occur to me. One of them is the notion of the *kairos* moment, in the Holy Spirit-inspired moment. You cannot go against it. You go against it, you will lose out, and I believe in terms of racial justice we are in a *kairos* moment. Anything you read, especially from Quakers in this country and America, is positive, forward-looking.... I'm going to have a meeting tonight with Black and Brown Quakers to discuss issues. We discussed about apologies last time and we're continuing with the debate. But equally this moment, a *kairos* moment, you can't stop it. I just got an email from Fred Ashmore. You know Fred Ashmore?

JD: I think the name rings a bell....

NN: He's Clerk to London Quakers.

JD: Okay, okay.

NN: So there's some work going on, and he was telling me I need to get in touch with somebody else who is doing some work... this is a *kairos* moment... I woke up this morning feeling great when I heard Biden is appointing the first openly gay Cabinet minister, Pete Buttigieg – their first![1] We are seeing the seeds that have been sown along the way. What we need, it seems to me, is to know how to move this work on in three different ways. For fellow travellers, recognition, encouraging them, giving them new ways, books, ways of thinking, even suggesting ways of meeting online, annual conferences, *anything*.

Then we write it in a way that encourages the other third to say, 'This is something you don't want to be left behind with, because you need to look deeply into it.' And to the third group we give a warning: 'You are doing a disservice both to yourself and to friends by holding your position.' I think it's where in a small contribution, you are speaking to the three constituencies in ways that will encourage debate. Totally different types of debate.

For me, anything I read now, in Britain Yearly Meeting, anything coming from America, Australia, New Zealand, South Africa, it's all positive. People have arrived. They'll be pulled back by the last one-third, because those people... will try to sabotage it, because they have not bought into the vision. The final one-third is unconscious, I believe. So for me it's knowing that whatever is happening, you can't stop it. There is a movement that is positive.

Now, of course you're an artist, you understand symbolism is very important, and that is the symbolism of changing names at Friends House, of recommending the bookshop to start carrying certain books that it hasn't carried before, the café to start thinking of offering different refreshments. It's about how you make a statement, and if you look at what I said about de-tribalising, I was saying you've got to do *things*... they are very small things you do, whether you're wearing a T-shirt or something, or you have an object in your house – what objects could we have in our MHs? What paintings? Things that would be speaking and saying there is a new dispensation which is not only in our *minds*. When you walk into this place, the place *speaks* a different language or an additional language. Otherwise, it's the same old, old story.

Meaningful Objects

JD: That reminds me that we've previously spoken about using and discussing objects and what they reveal about race relations, British-Kenyan relations or whatever, and I wonder if, in the future that might be a profitable way forward, because in terms of the symbolism and the sheer *tactility* of that object, that is a very good method of learning. You know it was a brilliant idea to bring that across from *A History of the World in 100 Objects*, [*referring to NN's project on de-tribalizing Kenya through discussing objects*] and bring it into a particular subject and use the same approach. I think that would be a very beneficial way forward. Just as an example, for British-Kenyan relations.... I remember when my family and I were over in Nairobi, we went to the National Museum, and they had – I'm sure you're very familiar with it – a brilliant display about the developing colonial relations between Britain and Kenya.

There were quite a few interesting objects, I mean, I'll never forget there was this particular photograph of White Kenyans, White Britons in Kenya during the 1952–60 Mau Mau Rebellion, who were marching against the Mau Mau, and my wife looked at the faces, and so many of them were wearing dark shades over their eyes, such hard faces. They just seemed so unsympathetic. In the event that you and I were ever to do something like that, a project of discussing culturally significant objects, that photograph would be one of my objects that I would suggest, because it just captured for me this sense of aggrieved *self-righteousness* [*he laughs*] on the part of these people who were the exploiters. [*They laugh.*] You know what I mean? And they were seeking to present themselves as the injured party and staging some sort of a fight-back, and in fact it was all topsy-turvy, they had it all upside down and the wrong way around, but that all came from their particular world-view. That photo really captured that moment.

NN: And in Kenyan terms, the Whites were saying, 'We were given this country in perpetuity by the British Government'! [*He laughs.*]

Twinning Toilets Is Good... but Not Enough!

NN: One of the things that occurs to me when we talk about symbolism... many Meetings have twinned toilets, and they have these framed pictures, twinned with this toilet, here, there.... I'd like to see Meeting twinning. You're twinned with *people*, it's not a picture that was put there ten years ago – that doesn't say anything. We want to know, during this Covid time, what's happening with the *community* you are *twinned* with? Do you have a named person in your Meeting, who liaises on behalf of the Meeting with these people, this Meeting? I mean, you can know through Friends' World Committee for Consultation, but this *twinning* action is where you can say, 'We can move from toilet to Meeting, from a mute object to people.' This is why I was saying that I felt good about Nottingham Meeting wanting to get in touch with Nairobi Meeting, and they were saying, 'We know they are programmed and there might be issues.' But I think I'll put them with both the programmed and unprogrammed. Part of the twinning symbolism is when cities initially say, 'We are twinned with a German city, with Tokyo!'

Then it can happen, that people go beyond just saying, 'We have tourists from these places that come.' There is an ongoing relationship of sorts. That's one thing we can put out there. In terms of symbolism, relationships that are ongoing, encapsulated in twinning with Meetings rather than a small thing, like toilets.... By the way, I think the toilets *are* very important, but we also need to go beyond that, we need *both*, toilet twinning and Meeting twinning – we need to go beyond toilets!

JD: That's really interesting.

NN: Because my question is: Why is diversity seen by some in our Quaker community as a threat rather than an opportunity, and what can we do about that? So it's very much what we've been talking about, that there are some... again not all Meetings see it as a threat, at least one-third see it as a good opportunity, one-third may take an ambivalent view, the last one-third may see it as a threat. But when we come to look at cultural change and allyship, we'll probably capture a little more of that.

Unconscious Bias

JD: Okay. Did you hear on the news yesterday that the Equality and Human Rights Commission [EHRC] has brought a report out on unconscious bias training, the government has recently decided to suspend unconscious bias training in the Civil Service, because they claimed that research had shown that it hadn't had much of an impact, and Doyin Atewologun was having a really good discussion about it with Evan Davies on Radio 4 News yesterday. It seemed with this as well, that the government is wilfully being very neutral, and if they were called out, they would say, 'Oh, we're very supportive of it, but it's because it doesn't seem to have worked like that, that's why we're suspending it for now,' sort of thing, and yet my instinct would be, 'Okay, suspend that if it's not working, but you need to put something else in its place.' It's not about just suspending that; you've got to come with something else that you're going to *do* to address the situation. I just wondered if you'd heard about it....

NN: No, I hadn't heard about that. I'll try and pick that up, because I'm working with the magistracy at the moment. But equally, unconscious bias... the American Psychological Society, the British Psychological Society, all these big societies agree psychologically it *exists*. So when the governments say Unconscious Bias Training is not working, but it's agreed that these things exist psychologically, what constitutes 'not working'? Because your car isn't going to work if you put the wrong kind of petrol into it! The petrol tank is right, it actually does work with petrol. [*He laughs.*] It's just you put the wrong type in! It's about saying, at what point is it not working, who did the evaluation, how much did they believe in this thing? There are a whole lot of things I'd like to know as to how they arrived at that conclusion.

JD: Me too.

NN: Because that's similar to when they said racial awareness training didn't work, back in the early days. That's what I meant when I was talking about the action bit: is this a 'budget item'? If someone's saying, 'We're spending too much money here,' I'd like to know a little bit more than that.

3: The 'A' Word: Allyship, and Doing It Well
23 December, 2020

Nim's discussion point:
- Why do I want to be an ally?

Jonathan's discussion point:
- What does 'allyship' look and feel like? How to implement this effectively and manageably? What does it look like on an individual level? What does it look like on a systemic level?

Quakers' Historical Legacy...

NN: What have you decided in your Meeting about how to proceed about diversity and inclusion?

JD: Yes, well, we've got a Business Meeting coming up on 3 January. At the moment it's proceeding a little bit *ad hoc*. This one Friend, who's doing a History degree, has put together a document on William Penn. She's put that together, we had a talk about it, now we've agreed that I can put that material into a PowerPoint which could be used to provoke a conversation. Then also, I've tried reaching out to one or two BAME colleagues. I'm in touch with the lead chaplain at the local hospital. I've now reached out to another colleague, a church pastor, who's a Nigerian doctor. Alongside that, it's sort of inter-related, I guess, we're doing a bit of work on the QLCC Gender Diversity statement.

...and Parallels with LGBTQ Issues

JD: We have a lesbian couple at our Meeting, and there's also someone who identifies as agender. They've talked about that over a period of weeks, and they've put together a statement about their experiences, and that's coming back to the Meeting at the same time. I just mention that because, in the light of what we said last week, it's all holistically interconnected.

It's not exactly the same thing, but they're a little bit in parallel, so we'll be discussing that in our Meeting. We'll report back on what we've done so far on race relations and race issues as well. I don't know if you've got any thoughts about whether that's the right kind of thing that we're doing.

NN: As I have said to other groups who have worked and talked about this, the challenge is always how do you get the balance between self-transformation and head-knowledge. All that information you pull together and present to people, you could on the one hand call it head-knowledge. It says, 'Now I know that which I didn't know yesterday about these topics.' About this person, about this epoch. And then... what? Or even sometimes, 'So what?!' [*They chuckle.*] Because they're so happy, now that they've read that book.... One client that I've seen in therapy... she had thirty self-help books, *thirty* in her library. I said, 'Which ones have you actually read through and *done* what they have asked you to do?' [*They laugh.*] 'I haven't done any.' I said, 'You spend money coming to me, and money buying these books, and what I tell you, you don't do, and what these books tell you, you don't do. Now let's see what stops you from doing the right thing you know you should, you could do, you must do.

So that is why with groups the challenge is, I give them information, they have the right to know this information, it's good to know this information, and then what do we do with it? Yesterday I was speaking with a very high-up Quaker in many ways, and he was giving me his diversity credentials, how he has moved far on. And I said to him, 'I have a problem with what you are telling me, Friend, because what you're telling me is so credible and good, but if it did not form part of your breakfast or dinner table conversation when you were growing up, if none of this was part of your primary socialisation, at home, secondary socialisation at school, or church, or Boy Scouts, when did you *un-learn* all that you learned that didn't have what you're telling me? You know what I mean? [*Chuckles*.] Because I was *never* taught about gay or lesbian relationships... that was *never* a conversation. So the question is, '*When* did I *un-learn* the negatives that I had learned?' Because all the conversation would have been negative: 'These poofters....' And so on.

I remember in 1991, we had a gay person who came to volunteer at the residential place I was running up in East London, and he said to me, 'Nim, I've got to be absolutely honest with you before I volunteer here, because many people have interviewed me and have not accepted me. I'm White, I'm gay, I'm HIV-positive.' And I said, 'If you pass the interview, that is immaterial to me.' And that's what he did. He passed the interview. One of my other workers, a Black, single mother, could not work with him. I talked with her, my deputy talked with her, about how we could re-arrange our work patterns so that she could accommodate him, and in the end she refused. I had to sack her. She's the one who used the word to me, 'You are sacking a single parent Black woman to accommodate a poofter.' And I remember that I said, '*Yes* – you know how hard it is for me to *do* that? Because I'm also the Chair of the Black Workers' Support Group! And now I'm having to justify that.' Twenty years later, one Sunday morning, I get a call, and somebody says, 'You don't know me, you haven't met me. My partner, Gary, before he died, wanted me to find you and say, ten years ago he remembered what you did, and on his death bed he wanted you to know that he remembered that.'

One has to arrive at the point where you un-learn the past. The weighty Quaker I was talking to yesterday, he did mellow a bit, and came a few notches away from his perspective, because I was saying, most of the things we have to un-learn, we were never taught the radical perspective that we may later identify and want to internalise. The receptacle that should accommodate new learning and is almost overflowing with the old learning. The question is, this information that I'm giving you, or you give to people, I give to people, are you filling that which is already full to overflowing, or are you *seeing it differently*? Part of that is, do you have the hunger and the thirst to know, to engage? Where is the motivation? If there is motivation, you will do it. You might ask some people why they're involved in Black Lives Matter. Some of it is head-knowledge, and that's fine.... If that's the level of your engagement, fine, at least you're engaging! For some people it is a continuum from head-knowledge and awareness to where that awareness leads you to action, and that action leads you to personal commitment, commitment in the Meeting, then society-wide, up to where you start challenging systemic racism and marginalisation. But wherever you're starting from, it's a long journey. We have to be clear what we are giving and sharing with people. But I wish you well. When we look back on this sort of journey it's always challenging, new learning, we don't *arrive*....

A Journey, Not an Arrival

JD: That's true. You've arrived if you're on the path....

NN: Yes. Because it's a process. You'll hear from not just Quakers, other groups where they say, 'Oh, we've done that, we've had a workshop.' This is not about an *event*. It's not about a weekend. [*He chuckles.*] It's an ongoing lifestyle change, about *becoming*, not *doing*....

JD: I agree with everything you say and I'm just aware, at our Meeting, at the moment, ethnically-speaking everyone is White, of one kind or another, mainly White British, maybe White European or whatever, but we don't have any explicitly BAME members, so I'm aware and I think my friend at the Meeting is aware, that there is a danger. She's gone off and done this really good historical research, and we're working on it and putting something together, to help them to start thinking about it, but

I think we're both aware that we're doing it as White people, but we don't want to be arrogant, really, and we're aware that there's a lot that we won't know or understand.... So we're aware that there are potential pitfalls for us just blithely going along and doing our own thing.... So I suppose that we're both quite keen if we can to invite someone, a BAME friend and colleague in, that would be a good thing. Would you say that's absolutely vital for us to do?

NN: I don't see it that way. You see, in the eighties I used to run a men's group. Black and White. Eight men. What we had in common, we had realised we were either married to, going out with, or were partnered with women who would identify themselves as Feminist. Now, we loved these women, the sensitivity that they were looking for from us, it seemed to us could easily come from gay men, but we were not gay. Neither were we macho men; we were very clear about that. If we were macho men, we wouldn't be with these women. If we were gay men, we wouldn't be with these women. So, who then were we? Part of this group, what we did was we each wrote letters to these women whom we loved, but who we found difficult in some way. Sometimes they curtailed our conversation, our openness, our awareness. Sometimes we found their challenges demeaning, etcetera. But we dared not send these letters to them. We only shared among ourselves, but what that did, a group of men talking about women and coming to terms.... We could have a man saying to another, 'Oh don't worry about that. I had the same fears before. This is how I handled it.' So somebody got support, encouragement, 'You should talk to so-and-so, read this, why don't you try this approach?'

In the end we disbanded, but we had successfully resolved our 'men issues'. Men issues around women resolved by men without the women concerned being present, and therefore when we left there, we went on our way well-armed to be able to carry on the conversation. For me, this is why with Woodbrooke there are all-White groups, concerned about this issue. It could be about anything – climate change, or gay, lesbian, and trans rights. You're saying, 'As novices on this, we are keen, we are open to exploring... not just about the *issue* – also ourselves and our views, what we think and feel, what we *know*. What challenges there are from what we're hearing....' It would be a brilliant group if it was facilitated well, where you said, 'As a White Meeting, what are the challenges presented by Black Lives Matter? We see these monuments coming down, we see marches, we hear things. Where do we stand? What do we think about this?'

We're saying also that there may come a time when we say, 'Can we invite somebody from the BAME community?' By that time you are inviting them either with a specific topic in mind, or you're inviting them having told them where you are and where you think you should be going. For me, it's thinking it's alright as an authentic group. If somebody wants to sit there, if you find a relevant person and say, 'We want you to sit as an observer. We don't want you to participate. We want you to *observe*. At some point we will ask you questions about what you have observed and how you are responding to it. You are not giving us more information, you are not telling us a history, you are not telling us about your own personal struggles [*he chuckles*]. We are saying you have listened to what we have said – what is your response?' That's what I'm doing with one Quaker Meeting now.

I'm currently involved with an all-White group at Woodbrooke. They had been challenged. They picked a piece up from a Black group in Philadelphia for 2020, and they're now working through their challenge. It really is okay for a group of people who are concerned to say, 'Before we can embark widely, we want to prepare.' It's almost like what we used to call in the old days in the Baptist Church a 'Pre-vangelism' meeting. Pre-vangelism. [*JD chuckles.*] Before you go there and evangelise [*they laugh*] you are 'pre'. Also, I can say that you're quite a resourceful person yourself. I'm sure you have enough there to make a start.

JD: Okay, thanks. Well, once I've got the PowerPoint knocked into shape, I may send you a copy, to hear what you think.

NN: Oh, yes, sure, I'll be glad to do that.

How We Present Is as Important as What We Are Presenting

NN: As I say, it's how you interpret things. I'll digress here a little. I did something for the Royal Air Force, at Hendon, in their museum. The African contribution to the First and Second World Wars. But again, it's just a small presentation, but it's *how* you present it. This is factual, but how do I present the facts so that they're not just caught in history, but they have relevance for today? You need to know this, but you need to know this because it has implications for today. And that's what I did for the Royal Air Force Museum, because Black history *happened*. When they say, 'You had a Black person flying a plane in 1915?' 'Yes!' [*They chuckle.*] Where else have they been recognised? You do your research and say, 'This is hidden history that I'm bringing upfront.' That is part of consciousness raising. I didn't know when I woke up this morning that people in your Meeting would say a particular thing. At the end of the Meeting, they know things that they didn't know before. Therefore, what do you do with that knowledge? With the Hendon Museum, it's saying every October when we have Black History Month, we've got all these schools, and kids come here and look, and they started asking, 'Didn't we, Black people, do anything?' That's why when they put out the word, I said I'd be interested to contribute.

JD: Excellent. Okay. We're up to Question 3 on allyship. I was wondering if maybe you'd like to do your question first this week, Nim, because the last two weeks I kicked off with my one and two.

Being an Ally

NN: I think the central thing for me is about getting somebody to have a conversation with themselves about, 'Why do I want to be an ally?' The need, the desire is there. I want to be an ally, meaning I want to walk alongside people, so that I can contribute something I have that will better their lives, which could be socio-political, environmental experience, whatever. For me, an ally who has a servant-leadership mentality which comes from what Christ said when washing the feet of the disciples – 'I didn't come here to be served but to serve.' That's a major mental shift.

Servant leadership isn't about one-upmanship, it's the capacity to affirm other people. You may *know* more than they do, you may be richer than them, you may have more things than they have, but how do you walk *alongside* a person? You've seen some of my examples of allyship, some people come up with superior attitudes, as if they are doing something *for* these people. If you don't see yourself as *implicated*.... The reason I am in this position of needing an ally is because you are implicated by being in the position where you *don't* need an ally. The question is, what *kind* of an ally are you? What motivates you? What are the gaps in your allyship perspective? What is it you want *me* to do for *you*? Because it's not just you [*he chuckles*] doing it for me. That's where some allyship makes you into a beggar. That you're an empty vessel – I have come to do for you that which you cannot do for yourself, and I want to say that I want you to come because you are the right person to remove obstacles that I can't even get near in order to remove them. But you have what it takes to go there and remove the obstacles. That for me is an ally. You have understood my condition. You have understood my obstacles, and not just projected them onto me the person. It's not just because of your colour. There are systemic, historical factors.... All that intersectionality of prejudices.

So for me an ally is a person that considers policies, projects, mentalities. Take Friends House, the café – what does the menu say? This is just a one-dimensional menu; who are you catering for? When you look at the pictures, what pictures are they? What do they tell us? If I come to a room, I want to see pictures that represent other people. It's an ally who has that wider concept, and it's my body, soul, and spirit that are seeing, tasting, hearing, touching... it's all those things. An ally becomes a kindred spirit, they become a fellow-traveller, an implicated person. In the nineties we used to help in gay marches, with the banners. I'm not gay, but my friend is. At that time that was such a powerful statement. When the Anglican Gay and Lesbian organisation asked me to serve on their committee because they really didn't have anybody from ethnic minorities they could approach, I knew what they were talking about. I could remove some barriers for them by talking to Black people who viewed me as a credible person, whereas the first thing that they would see about LGBTQ Christians was that they were White, talking about gay people. But BAME people would see me as 'one of us'. Perhaps misguided, but they'd say, 'At least let us listen to what he has to say.' [*He chuckles.*]

It is that bit, an ally who removes barriers that impede progress and they have the wherewithal because of their position in life to do that, but they don't count that as something that they're doing *for* people, they are doing it *with* people, because they are implicated. That's what I can say about that, Jonathan.

Paulo Freire, Conscientization and Solidarity

JD: Can I throw something in here? Listening to you saying all of that, it takes me back to Paulo Freire, and *conscientization* and solidarity and his point that the teacher is supporting the students. You yourself made this point previously, but the students must free *themselves* with the teacher's solidarity and support. They must actively free themselves, it's not about the teacher doing that *for* them or *to* them but rather *beside* them, working *with* them. That was one thing that jumped into my head. And – forgive me, because I've been vaguely familiar with this term 'intersectionality', and you used that in a phrase, 'intersectionality of prejudices'. I scribbled that down, but then I also wrote, 'but also of interests' and that seemed to chime with what you went on to say, that it's not one person doing something for another, it's both doing it together. We have lots of vicious circles in our society, but I remember saying before how beneficial it can be if what people enjoy doing or would like to do can be associated with good things as well. That's one way of creating that 'virtuous circle'.

You talk about it – I read your article[1] again last night, and I'd already highlighted some bits and I found myself highlighting more... you made that point as well here, in quoting Martin Luther King, where he talks about how each person's potential to become an integrated fully-developed person is dependent upon other people becoming integrated and fully-developed people as well. I *cannot* be fully developed if my brothers and sisters are not fully developed.

NN: Yes.

Intersectionality

JD: This feeds back into this awareness that's been growing in me, and again you've been saying this, and it's coming to the fore in my mind again, based on what you've been saying, that it's all holistic. It's not about someone *just* being an environmentalist, or a Feminist, or a gay rights activist, or an anti-racist campaigner, or any one of those things. If you support gay rights, you've got to support the rights of BAME people, you've got to support women's rights and so forth. It's all interconnected - intersectional. I've thought about that over this last week, it's so important.... I'm also aware when I *think* it, this category that you identify in your article, particularly... the 'proxy allies', superficial allies. I hear in my head a proxy ally saying, 'Well, that's all true [*they chuckle*] but it's so *big*! How can I possibly get my head around it? I don't know where to start, so I won't do anything at all.... But you've got all my moral support and my emotional agreement (!) I'm standing here agreeing with you, but I just don't know where to start, because it's so massive.' But then I realised that even as I hear that question, I then remember... you've said it in our conversations, and I have it written here: 'What can you do to further the cause of social, racial and environmental justice *within your own sphere of influence*?'

When I was teaching, I liked to have quotes up around my wall, various inspirational quotes. One of them was from Arthur Ashe – you'll know him of course – the first Black male player to win Wimbledon. When people asked him, 'How did you manage this? You triumphed over so much,' he said, 'Start where you are. Use what you have. Do what you can.' I really like that. It's a great mantra for anyone wanting to achieve something, and it's certainly good for students, I think. You don't have to look and think it's a massive long road, it's a massive achievement that I want to ultimately reach, how do I get there? Just start where you are, use what you have to hand, do what you *can* with it at this moment, and just keep on doing that little by little.

Staying Conscious

JD: Now that all links back in with when I reminded myself of my question; perhaps it overlaps with yours? What does allyship look and feel like? How to implement this effectively and manageably? What does it look like on an individual level? What does it look like on a systemic level? That's crystallized in my head the question, what tangible things can be said and done, what tangible symbols and images could there be to keep people inspired and to support them in remaining *conscientized*, keeping the key issues at the front of their minds, and being comfortable with discomfort?

NN: Two things come to mind. One is most well-informed people, amongst Friends and activists, you know when you're doing something for the environment, you're not doing it for anybody in particular – you are doing it for *us*. All of us. Society. We all have little bits that we do, and it's our little bits that contribute to the big bits. I see the same thing on diversity and inclusion and the whole intersectional wholeness movement. It's saying you are doing it for the sake of humanity and you are doing the bit that you can, because the big picture is so big.

Now, the second thing is what I do with the one-third of like-minded people. First all, I identify people, named individuals. On 7 January I'm going to sit with a group – I've never sat with them before, I've only met one person who is in this group. They are called 'the Council'. A long time ago, people used to sit down and talk about things, to support each other. So I'm going to see what they are about. Talking to my contact from this group, I knew that he is one of the one-third like-minded. When he sent me an email, we connected a lot. My area of responsibility, with fellow-travellers, is to encourage movement from 'I am doing…' to 'We are doing…' and part of this 'We are doing…' could be the activity but also trying to get the second one-third interested in becoming part of what we're doing. You are *doing* something. I don't have to depend on you to do my bit. But outside of my area of responsibility I need you to do something so that our area expands, and we get more people to become involved…. That's why if we write these articles we will have *expanded*, and we will get other people responding. One-third will say, 'Great!' One-third will say, 'Oh, I don't know about this….' [*He chuckles.*] The other one-third will say, 'I don't like it.' But we're doing something. That's the way I see it. I'm saying that it seems to me that you're on the right course. You are doing, you are working…. How do I translate head-knowledge into practical, lived experience for the sake of humanity? Not for the sake of Black people. Not for the sake of women. For the sake of humanity.

Freedom for All

JD: That's exactly right, because Freire also says that when the oppressed are freed, that frees the oppressors as well. The oppressors are just as oppressed as those they oppress, just in a different way. I'm trying to do my little bit, not *for* other people. Or rather, it is partly for other people, but it's also for myself. In doing it, I'm also helping myself. It's that co-lateral, interactive, dialogical part of it that's very important, and maybe that's something that will feed into anything that we write, that in contributing in a small way to someone else's freedom you're actually freeing yourself as well.

NN: Yes! I can never be fully me unless and until you are fully you. I will go through life short-changed in some way if there is another short-changed human who I need to walk alongside. Because if you walk alongside somebody who is falling behind and you leave them, can you really leave another human being behind and forget them, because they aren't keeping up, and you have the wherewithal to help them? The other thing that this reminds me of is something I always used to find silly in some sense, but you'd have some people saying 'She married beneath herself', or 'He married beneath himself'. [*He chuckles.*] I always used to ask, 'This man, this woman, they go out, or man and man, woman and woman, and they fall in love.' The criteria for their life together is that they are in love, yet there are other people, who will bring alien concepts and say, 'She's married someone shorter, taller, Black, less educated, whatever... "beneath themselves".' It always reminds me when I talk about race issues, some people see this whole thing as 'beneath themselves'.... If you don't see this as beneath yourself, then you will see how you are implicated.

Kenya and the British Empire

JD: I raised my awareness a little when we visited Kenya and we heard more about the history of the British Empire there, and reading a bit more about it. I felt horror when I realised exactly what the British forces did, what we, the British, perpetrated in Kenya. I realised that there it was, it's something that sits on the record. It's *there*.

But it hardly ever gets spoken of, and that's a way of suppressing it. It's shameful, and I did feel, because I was the White Briton, I felt ashamed. There was this horrible thought, when I was growing up particularly, but still now.... When people were talking about the Second World War, quite rightly, people would look at what was done in the Holocaust, in the Final Solution, by the Nazis, and it was evil, it was despicable, everything. But there was a moral comfort in projecting that out onto the Nazis, and thinking, '*They* did all those terrible things, they were bad people.' But then I looked at what was perpetrated in Kenya, and I thought, the one thing that we didn't do to Black Kenyans, was to put them in gas chambers. But we did pretty much everything else that the Nazis did to the Jews and other minorities. It's uncomfortable to realise that, it's a big issue and you, I, we need to start picking away at that. I'm sure at some stage I'm going to have to write something about it, whatever form that might take, a story or an article or whatever, but I'm going to have to try and make a little contribution to opening that up so that people are more aware of it and start to try to deal with it.

NN: When you say that, Jonathan, I'm sure you've found that part of it is the British saying, 'These Kenyans are the other, they are beneath us.' That's what I was saying about 'marrying beneath'. Sometimes you keep pulling rank. Interestingly, I have somewhere in my papers a document from 1700-and-something, where you could get a licence to shoot kangaroos and Aborigines. When I came across it some years ago, I couldn't believe it! You have a licence, and this other person's humanity is so negated, you could come and say, 'I've shot ten kangaroos and five Aborigines' and that, in polite company, was acceptable. It would be good to think about writing something about that, I think.

I collect a lot of books from Kenya. The earliest was written in 1905. Quite a number of racist works but equally there were quite a number of good British people who supported social and racial justice and are remembered with affection... have a look for the BBC documentary of David Steel going to Kenya and talking to working class people who knew him when he was a boy and knew his father. You can see he's in tears, and other people, because he was one of those people recognised as a good person. It's almost as if he were a good person who happened to be White! [*They laugh.*] Amongst bad White people.

JD: When we were there in Kenya, when we were driving around with our hosts, several times we drove past White Kenyans... people who were born and raised in Kenya who are resident there still.

NN: Kenya Cowboys. That's how they are known in the media, yes. [*He laughs.*]

JD: Oh, interesting, okay. Well, the chap who was driving us would honk his horn and wave at them, and one time he said, 'The chap we just saw, he's a doctor in one of the hospitals in Nairobi,' and he spoke very, very warmly about the White people who he knew, and it's obvious that there are White people out there trying to do their bit as well, which is good.

NN: Yes, especially the ones who stayed. You see, I'm on the border of Kenyan society here, and again we have a third Black Kenyans, a third White Kenyans, a third Asian Kenyans. These are people who love the country, they love the people, and those are the ones who stayed or who have homes there, family.... I see that our hour is gone.

4: Hidden Gems: Finding Them, and What to Do with Them
30 December, 2020

Jonathan's discussion point:
- How might we understand the concept of 'holisticity', both in terms of how negative factors are intimately bound up within the weave of our lives and so are difficult to unravel, but also the importance of taking a holistic approach to weaving in positive changes and attitudes within our everyday lives? One area is:
  - History (the complexity of unpicking motives, actions, attitudes, and balancing this against an awareness of shifting attitudes and values)

Nim's discussion point:
- How to reconcile intersecting forces of oppression?

Living Inside-out

We began by discussing an article by Nim in the Spiritual Directors Network (SPIDIR) newsletter,[1] going on to talk about the anthology Black Fire. *They discussed a quote from Jean Toomer, in 'Keep the Inward Watch', one of his anthologised pieces in that book: 'Why is it so difficult for us to go in and become able, in the words of Douglas Steere, "to live for the inside, outwards, as whole men?"'*

NN: Yes, the living inside-out…. That only happens if one is very well centred, cautiously aware, one has *transformed*, because this is more than *change*, this is transformation. Change happens through therapy and all that, transformation comes through interaction with the Spirit. It is that transformation that makes you work from the inside out, where you then don't endow people with more positive or negative capacities than they have. I can always remember when I was training very early on in therapy and beginning to practise, especially meeting young people in relationships where somebody was endowing the other person with qualities that they didn't possess. It was like loving yourself through them. Because you yourself are not centred. Equally, endowing them with negative emotions which you then come to hate, it's almost like hating yourself through them. Which is the whole concept in Psychology of transference and counter-transference. You transfer all the negatives and distance yourself from those negatives and therefore hate the person who becomes a carrier. [*He laughs.*] Which isn't a Christian notion of atonement.

The Ancient Jews, took this goat, and endowed it with all the sins of the nation and it was sent out into the wilderness, and then for the next whole year you were clean because the sins had been carried out by this animal. It's the claim of Jesus that 'I'm hanging on the cross, I'm *absorbing*'. Now Jesus is saying, 'I have absorbed, therefore don't hate yourself, *centre* yourself.' I always find that, it's the same concept with demonising. We demonise – 'I cannot be like that!' Yet the same skeletons we have in our cupboards that we don't bring out, we hang on other people. Our topic today is, 'How do we proceed with our quest for diversity and inclusion among Friends without inflicting guilt or shame? How do we demonstrate a profound love and respect for who they are, as they are?' I think that part of that is…. If I wait for my fellow human beings to be fully formed, in order for me to love them, I'll be waiting until the end of time. So I think for me, again I go back to the three thirds. I am clear that not everyone wants to be included in the new dispensation. Some people, they're tired, they have other fights to fight and the whole issue of diversity and inclusion on the priority list is very low, and I've got to accept that.

Historical Legacies

NN: The person who decides to go to an AA meeting instead of going to a demonstration or a meeting where they're talking about diversity, I understand their priority, but I cannot just let them be without a conversation. Because without a conversation there can never be intimacy. In order to create trust, in order to walk alongside one another, if I'm low in your priorities and the only help you can give is to write a cheque, that's it. You are involved, you are implicated. But you are not at the forefront, and I sometimes think about religious people and specifically Quakers on the issue of inclusion and diversity, and I look at the thirteen disciples, because we had twelve then there was the one who replaced Judas. How many of those do we hear about in popular culture? How many wrote their Gospels? History tells us almost all of them except John at Patmos became martyrs and History tells us more than the Gospels tell us about them. Therefore, what we popularly know about those disciples who were at the forefront, who thought and wrote, those are the ones who we interact with via their narratives and Gospels, and they become the ones who form our world view about ourselves, others and God.

But the majority didn't write anything that they left behind, that was included in the official canon. But they did do much better work than they are sometimes credited for, and it is the same thing, you have narratives from marginalised people that are powerful but we are never told about them. For me, that bit of where and when you ask about how we proceed with our quest for diversity and inclusion amongst Friends, is first of all uncovering these hidden gems, hidden history, denied histories of Friends in the past, Blacks in the past, and saying they were not always enslaved, they've been much more than that. They are hidden histories, just like the hidden histories of disciples that we never get to hear. You have to go deep and seek from other sources than the common canon. Therefore, this common canon, whether it is a Quaker common canon or whatever common canon is out there in the market place, that is the one that is given prominence and it's for us to say in terms of what we're talking about in our conversation, there are canons that are hidden, they are equally valid and powerful, and we are short changing ourselves as a Society of Friends and as a world if these ones are not included.

Helen Morgan Brooks and Ethical Writing

JD: I think that point is great, that chimes with something else that happened with me this week. As I was reading *Black Fire* one of the people included there is Helen Morgan Brooks, who was a little bit on my radar because she came up in my research for my MA. She features in an essay by Diane Reynolds, 'Quakers and Fiction: Towards Breaking out of the Backward Gaze' included in a book called *Quakers and Literature*. Reynolds is making a case for Quaker writers to engage in what she calls 'ethical writing', which for her is unsentimental, morally, ethically, politically honest. Broad-minded. Unflinching in accepting the dark as well as the light. She uses Morgan Brooks as one of the writers who she credits as practising this, and she quotes some of her poetry in the essay. I brought Brooks in as one example of someone it would be good to explore if anyone wanted to develop the ideas in my dissertation further, and look at different categories of Quaker experience other than the two Quaker writers who I looked at in my dissertation.

NN: Yeah.

JD: I've been really impressed by the poetry that I read in *Black Fire*, then it sent me back to Reynolds, and I started digging around, looking for what was out there on Brooks. It struck me, there isn't a huge amount. I think Reynolds' inclusion of her in this essay is one of very few pieces of critical work on Helen Morgan Brooks. I don't know how available her poetry is in Britain, and it struck me, going back to what you were saying last week about doing what we can in our own contexts, that's what we need to do. Of course, it's fenced around with issues and pitfalls, and you have to be very careful how you critically analyse other people's work, especially if they don't belong to the same social, cultural, economic, ethnic milieu as yourself, but it did strike me that maybe this is something I *can* constructively do. I could certainly enjoy conducting some research about Helen Morgan Brooks, and putting something together on her life and work. Anyway, I thought I'd put that in now. That might be something I could perhaps do, and I might be able to expand people's awareness of her, because she's a really good poet, I think. She writes across a whole range of experiences, just the little flavour you get in *Black Fire*, she writes about Quaker spiritual experience, then she's writing about the experience of under-privileged people, the slums and ghettoes, what that was like. It's all there, it's very expansive work that she's doing, I think.

NN: Yes, I think that that is part of the hidden or unknown not given the prominence that it should receive, and that will be interesting at some point, if we could compile a list of publications that we could send to the bookshop at Friends House, or even persuade the editors of *The Friend*, to have a page of these books, saying why we are recommending that people buy them and the Bookshop stock them.

JD: We could even – it depends how extensive the list is – but there's scope there to do some small pieces on some of these different writers, on their lives and work, discussing why they're so important.

NN: Yes. That is actually something we could think about, have on the back-burner, because if we aim to a) recommend these books, and b) even started a reading group of these books, it would mean that we are expanding the circle. We might get that one-third who are kindred spirits and others who want to join, and very clearly it would be an article saying, 'We are setting up a reading group specifically for these books, these types of books and that would be something non-threatening, for people who like reading and discussing books but equally might be challenged, but in a safe space.' I think that's something that we could probably try during the summer.

Loving Yourself, Loving Others

NN: The second part of that question, how do we demonstrate a profound love and respect for who they are as they are, that's what you mentioned at the beginning of this conversation, it's got to come inside out. This is not something one puts on one's self. We can only have a profound love and acceptance of other people because we feel a profound love and acceptance of ourselves. You can't give what you don't have. The Africans have a saying, 'You can't draw sweet water from a bitter well.' [*He chuckles.*] You give what you have, but as Martin Luther King said, you can't do that without being part of a beloved community. You can't carry your cross all alone. This type of work means you carry your cross with others. As Paulo Freire found in his work with *conscientization*, you empower people, those marginalised farm workers, so-called uneducated, and part of the challenge is, originally, he thought once their consciousness was raised, they would behave right, ethically speaking.

Granted, they now had become liberated and found themselves in a better place, but some of them went on to become little oppressors, because they had internalised their oppression, just like some of the African leaders, they had internalised how the governor had behaved, lording it over people. If you see the president or the governor, in some developing countries, the motorcade, sometimes it's half a mile long! Motorcycles! Motorcades! All that – that was what they used to see the government doing. They internalised how to be powerful, how to handle power, how to suppress opponents. It is that bit where, this is not about once we get to power, as Blacks we'll oppress Whites, or women who oppress men, or gays who oppress straights. That type of thing doesn't work, because as we said last week, it's for the sake of humanity. We humanize the human race, we humanize our Friends, Quakers, but not naively. As a good Christian friend once used to tell me, the eleventh commandment is, 'A Christian is not a fool'! [*They chuckle.*] There is objective truth, and there is naivety, and we don't collude with the oppressors, the liars, the manipulators. Neither do we want to be turned into manipulators ourselves. It's where we regain our own humanity for the sake of humanity.

One of the other things I was thinking about while we were talking is one of the things I really regret not doing. I was at the South African Embassy for a memorial of Helen Suzman. One of the people who was there was Shirley Williams. She told me when we asked each other why we were there, she told me it was Helen Suzman who wrote to her very early on, when there were fewer than a dozen women parliamentarians in the world, and she called them into a meeting, saying 'We've got to be working together. We're all women parliamentarians, wherever we are. We have a perspective and a perception that we need to share more.' That's why she was there. Then we were talking about young people, she gave me her card and said, 'Get in touch. We'll talk about this.' I never did. That is one of my regrets. So having this other side, we need to listen to it. So that for the sake of humanity, Suzman said, 'Come together, as women, for the sake of humanity.' Not just for the poor, or women, or just for the sake of Blacks. The bottom line is, just like some people are into action without contemplation, and some people are into contemplation without action, what we are about has to be the fruits of contemplation and action as a symbiotic thing.

JD: That links in with some of these quotes as well, from your SPIDIR article, that I scribbled down: 'Christianity is an incarnational faith.' 'Separate action from contemplation in spiritual direction is disingenuous. Only a spirituality energised by the power of love with a strong social practical quest for the common good will suffice.' That's a key insight.

'Spiritual, mental and emotional maturity takes place over a lifetime, with each person travelling their unique road towards transformation.' I think you're right, Nim. I think that relates, certainly on a personal level, to my question about the notion of 'holisticity', both in terms of how negative factors are intimately bound up within the weave of our lives and so are difficult to unravel, but also the importance of taking a holistic approach to weaving in positive changes and attitudes within our everyday lives. The immediate area where this seems most pressing to me is History (the complexity of unpicking motives, actions, attitudes, and balancing this against an awareness of shifting attitudes and values).

Accepting Our Imperfections

JD: As you were talking, it made me wonder, maybe this is the moment... I mean, I'm not perfect, am I? It feels like a real privilege that you're making the time for us to have these conversations. I'm finding them really interesting and enjoyable and it's a great learning process for me, and, also, at the back of my mind I'm thinking this doesn't make me a good person, it makes me a lucky person, really. [*They laugh.*] I know that we're all a mix, and that goes for me as much as for anybody else. I know in the past there have been times when I've been ignorant or thoughtless or I've said and done or *not* said or done things, and I was in the wrong. I don't know if I need to admit some of that here. I don't know if that's appropriate or not. Perhaps I need to bring one or two moments that I recall, either into our conversations, to work with them. Or maybe I need to work on them, and they might find their way into one of the bits that I'm going to write as a result of all of this. I don't know if you have a view on that? I'm open to talking a little bit about that if you think it's the right thing to do.

NN: I think my first view is that you and I are in this conversation, not just because you and I chose the moment.

There is another *dimension* where we are meant to have this moment for our mutual benefit. Mutual learning, mutual benefit. I strongly believe it has a spiritual dimension, so it's not just about Jonathan and Nim sending each other emails and saying, 'Let's get together.' There is, if you want, a back-story, a behind-the-scenes activity of the Spirit. So again, another African saying: 'When the time comes, the baby must be born'! [*They laugh.*] Whether it is delayed, the time comes... This is all about trust and feeling comfortable with one another. If you feel there is enough trust and comfort to be able to go deeper. I'm sure you've come across those steps: forming, norming, storming, performing?

Moving from Norming to Storming

NN: All this time so far what we've been doing, it's been norming, and the norming stage comes to an end at some point, and you move on to the storming stage. That's where you start sharing hard things. You and I are personally implicated in *things*. These are not just objective, academic, out-there issues. That's where we start – and gradually we come to a point where we are *implicated*, and that's where we start looking at how we are being transformed by the conversation. That is going deeper. And a time will come where I will tell you, you'll tell me things that probably you've never told anybody. That's part of the journey. The thing is not to try to quicken the journey, neither to delay it. It's getting that balance. Part of it is you feeling comfortable. If it is there, and you feel it is a safe place, as I feel, just share.

JD: Okay. Thanks. It's come into my head a couple of times. I *feel* comfortable, so I'll plunge in.... There are three things in my head... I'll do the first one and we'll see. For my first degree I did English and American Literature. One event that was put on by a member of staff, extra to lectures and seminars, every month, there was an American Studies seminar. This member of staff would arrange for different people to give a talk, maybe from within the department, maybe from outside. Anyone who was interested could turn up, it wasn't for credit, just for enrichment. There were various topics to do with American Studies, and one time a Native American writer came to talk about his work and Native American issues. I'd been doing some reading on that, it was part of one of the courses that I was doing at the time, so I found it very interesting. Also, just to contextualise this, I'm half-Canadian, my dad's from Canada. My father's always been quite sympathetic to Native Canadians, and sympathetic about the things that have been done to them by White Canadian settlers as well, but I have to be honest, I'd absorbed the term 'Red Indian', which I don't think I've used since that day when I was eighteen, and being rather ignorant, without quite realising what I was doing, I asked a question of this man after his talk, and thoughtlessly used that term. No sooner was it out of my mouth than he very clearly looked at me and said, 'Native American'.

Then he carried on and responded to my question. I felt absolutely awful [*he laughs*] and ashamed. I felt dreadful. I went away feeling rotten, because I'd obviously offended this chap. I mean, he was just very clear with me that I'd misused language, and gave me the correct language to use.... Over time, that was sufficient, and I went away and thought about it.

Why am I mentioning it now? Because it's one key memory from my past that, when I look back, I still feel very uncomfortable about it. I felt bad. I'm sure in the grand scheme of things, other people have done things that were worse, but we're not talking about other people, we're talking about me.

It was an inappropriate thing to say, although genuinely at that moment if you'd pointed it out to me.... I was very ignorant. I certainly didn't say it to give offence. I suppose it was one of those necessary moments in my life where my unthinking, unconscious way of being came up against another person's more conscious way of being, and necessarily I felt guilty, embarrassed and all that, I went away and thought about it. I always use 'Native American', 'Native Canadian'.... It still makes me feel uncomfortable when I look back on it, actually, but also, yeah, we're not perfect, I'm not perfect....

NN: No one is, and in the first article I wrote for *The Friend*, when I was saying about bed, room, next-door housemates, there was one of them I described as 'naïve with no malice'. I am not ashamed if I am naïve with no malice because.... It seems to me that you're not saying that you knew the right terminology to use, and you refused to use it.

JD: No, it certainly wasn't a conscious decision. It was a knee-jerk use. It wasn't deliberately offensive.

NN: I don't think you would have chosen to... it would have been very odd for you to have chosen to embarrass yourself in front of everybody and this eminent person by using the wrong terminology knowingly. There's that bit where Jesus asks Simon Peter three times, 'Do you love me?' Peter says, 'You know everything.' He's almost saying, 'You know....' That moment of witness, of naivety, of fear, a deed which does not become me.

I once met a Native American leader called Chief Man Killer and asked for her autograph in my copy of her book. She's the one who Obama gave the freedom of the city. I remember her standing there on the podium and saying, 'None of you expected what some of you call a Red Indian chief to be a woman. Here I am, I'm a chief, and my name is Man Killer.' Fantastic. If you google her, she was a fantastic woman. She did acknowledge what we thought, which was being contradicted by this person, and I went up to speak to her and get her autograph. If you meet a person who is perfect, I think they are dead. We're still living. [*They laugh.*] Is your dad still alive?

JD: Yes, yes. He's in his late seventies now, but he is still alive, yeah....

We discussed Jonathan's family background in a little more detail....

NN: So, Jonathan, I quite understand, because you're saying at the age of eighteen that happened, and it must have had quite a profound effect upon you.... And this is where you are trying to deconstruct it, and this is because, for me, if a person is not trying to reinforce it, they're trying to deconstruct it, and that is what we should be doing with all these histories and the past.... I have my past which I try to deconstruct.... So, you have siblings?

We discussed Jonathan's relatives in some further detail....

NN: It's those dynamics, you have a multi-cultural base, I know there are similarities between Canada and the UK, but there are aspects specific to that background, and I like the saying that we are what we have been becoming with whom we've been journeying, and you've been journeying with your brother, your parents, and that's who we have been becoming and who we are.

JD: I think that's absolutely right. It's funny, isn't it? You become aware as you grow older... you see certain traits from your parents emerging in yourself. My father, when my brother and I were young, he used to drive us mad playing around with words, and we used to think it was really silly. He used to do it all the time. [*NN laughs.*] Now I find myself doing it with my son, [*they laugh*] so there you go. Sometimes my son laughs, and sometimes he finds it silly and annoying. So he'll probably do it when he's my age if he has children.

NN: That's what we're talking about, and I think part of what we were talking about last week, about primary socialisation. I told you I was saying to somebody, we never sat around our breakfast table talking about pro-Black, pro-gay issues. Those conversations didn't happen. Sometimes, those conversations happen in the negative and we internalize so much. This whole issue of unconscious bias, in positive and negative ways, is both real and powerful. I never understood tribalism, even when I was growing up. I can remember my mum one time saying to me, 'Son, over the years you've brought four girls to introduce to me. What about girls from our tribe? Don't you like girls from our tribe?' I didn't see them in those terms. Therefore, that way of looking, of being, translated to what I've been saying, whether it's race and racism, seeing the third way that comes from inter-dependence. I know you've got to grow to be there, but I cannot on the one hand be tribalistic and on the other be fighting for social justice. It's not a campaigning agenda, it's a being, just as we've been talking about. Are they involved with Quakers at all, your parents or your brother?

Our Quaker Backgrounds
JD: No. We had a fairly standard Anglican upbringing, really, my mum's Anglican. My dad was born and raised Lutheran. When I was younger, I thought of myself as an Anglican. I did dabble in other denominations. Increasingly through my twenties, I started to feel that I wasn't deriving all of what I needed from church services, but I was certain for me there was something there, and I wanted to find the right religious path for me.

NN: Yeah.

JD: Then when I was in my late twenties, I was aware of Quakers, they were on my radar. When he was at university, my brother attended Carlton Hill Meeting in Leeds. He was very impressed with it, talked to me about it. My mother had a Quaker friend, and she talked very highly of them. It all came to a head: I was talking about how I was looking for 'It', but I hadn't found 'It' yet, I wasn't even sure what 'It' was. Then my mother said, 'Maybe you need to try something other than Anglicanism', and my brother said, 'Well, maybe Quakerism is something you want to find more out about.' It all converged. I went to my local meeting in Muswell Hill, and I've never looked back. It's been great. Of course, we all have ups and downs, don't we? We have our dry periods, but I've never doubted that I'm a Quaker, and I love it. Actually, I went through a period where I became quite militant and cut myself off a little from other denominations. I think I needed to do that to establish myself as a Quaker.

NN: That's a bit of independence, isn't it? You're independent of them, but in the face of interdependence you're no longer caught up in one specific approach, but it's important to go through that independent phase where you concentrate on something.

JD: Mm. I do enjoy joining in other forms of worship now, which is good, yet Quaker worship is the defining rock for me. But that prompts me to ask how it has been for you? Are you still involved with the Baptists as well?

NN: No, but I'm ecumenical. I'm part of an accrediting body we are setting up for spiritual directors, and one of the people I've invited is a Baptist minister... I see myself very much as working ecumenically.

JD: Did you come to Quakers as an adult as I did?

NN: Only ten years ago. I've only been a Quaker for ten years.

JD: Ah, okay, okay. [*NN chuckles.*]

NN: After I'd had eighteen months of the dark night of the soul, looking for something, we did go to a Mennonite community, spent a day there. But they don't have a church close to us. We went to a local Quaker Meeting. I was still going as a visiting speaker to the Baptist Church, while attending Quakers, for about a year. When I knew I was moving towards Quakerism, that was it. I went to a weekend at Woodbrooke, then did the Equipping for Ministry course. That was a very good entry. It gave me time to think.

5: Enlarging the Tent: Ways of Dealing with Our (Dis)comfort Zones
6 January, 2021

Jonathan's discussion point:
- Continuing with the concept of 'holisticity', how can I move forward in terms of (Global) economic systems and how they hardwire privilege (and my complicity in them)?

Nim's discussion point:
- What's the best way of involving everyone to commit to 'speaking truth to power' in support of strengthening social cohesion?

Kenyan Possibilities
We began by chatting about the Christmas and New Year holidays.

JD: Could I ask, because I was just reading through the transcript again this morning, to polish it. Just out of interest, really, what subject does your wife teach at Harrow College?

NN: She teaches ESOL,[1] but she also teaches teachers to teach ESOL. Her MA was in teaching teachers. That is one thing we hope is transferable when we go to Kenya at some point.

JD: I'm sure it will be. Are you planning at some stage to relocate to Kenya?

NN: Yes, I mean it's one of those things that you wrestle with... two daughters here, they're still single, but quite happy, they live together, 30 and 32. My greatest thing is to start an art gallery in Kenya.

I've been collecting since the Nineties. I've got quite a good collection, and I have this great idea, whether it'll come to pass or not. We have very good carvers in Kenya. Wood carvers and stone carvers. There is the Kisii stone in Kenya. There are also very good carvers in Tanzania, the Makonde. And also in Congo. My idea is to find one.... I have collected items from every African country, and my idea is to do a replica. Some of them are in museums in Europe and around the world. Some of them are in Kenya. To do an object from every African country, then try to get contemporary artists to give us permission to make replicas, so you have an original object from the bygone age, and a contemporary one, and use that to create a training/ teaching arts project for Africa, so it'll be something accessible to the diaspora, to Africans, but tested in Kenya. So that, with 100 objects, those are the things you say to God, 'If that's what you want me to do, you've got to open the way.' I know how to open my *own* way! [*They chuckle.*] My own way is to sell eight acres of the land, and I'll get enough money to do the work, but that would be my own way, so I'm not sure yet.

JD: Best of luck with that. That sounds really interesting.

NN: Thank you... do you want to start today?

JD: It's the second part of my question from last week, about 'holisticity', the negative factors which are interwoven into the material of our lives, how difficult it is to unravel that, and the importance of a holistic approach to weaving positive factors into our lives. This second part of it is about (global) economic systems and how they hardwire privilege – and how I'm complicit with them.

I've put the two questions together and had a little think ahead of time. Yours, I know we'll come to that in a while, yours is broader but mine perhaps fits within it or there's some overlap between our questions. But we can come to that. This week particularly I was looking back over some reading I've been doing, and I don't know if it's serendipity or what, but it does seem that the flow of what we've been talking about seems to be building. Patterns and ideas keep rising up; interesting things are coming through. We've already been talking about how you build that positive momentum, how you start to find your allies, how you find the one-third who are natural allies, and the one-third who are more sympathetic.

Alongside that there's the issue of how you raise these difficult questions with some of the people you want to speak to and reach out to in such a way that they don't find it threatening. Or at least [*he chuckles*] they don't find it *so* threatening that they close down, so that they can become comfortable with being uncomfortable. That echoes from what you said last week about possibly putting together a list of publications for *The Friend* and Friends House bookshop, and maybe starting up some sort of a reading group and that kind of thing. That sparked off some ideas I've had, I've just scribbled them down, there are four or five of them. I want to go back before the moment's lost. Last week I mentioned about a quote I came across in the Jean Toomer section of *Black Fire*, living from within, inside-out.

The Inward Watch

JD: I've found the quote that I was referring to. It's within the section titled, 'Keep the Inward Watch'. We mentioned it last time: 'Why is it so difficult for us to go in and become able, in the words of Douglas Steere, "to live from the inside outwards, as whole men?".' He goes on, 'the way in is blocked.' He's very much taken with this idea that inside there are contrasts, and there's good and evil within us, and the good and evil have to contend. My understanding is, he sees that Lamb's War, that internal war, as burning the evil out of us, or allowing it to be burnt out of us, so that we become wholly good. So, that's a great quote, and maybe we can do something with it. That perhaps plays into, again, how we are going to facilitate that process for ourselves and other people. The next thing that I scribbled down was '*conscientization* of the privileged alongside the oppressed' and this idea that we were talking about, to liberate the oppressor is co-equally important with liberating the oppressed, and then both will be liberated by that process.

How is that presented? How do we create a process by which those people who are privileged and therefore complicit in the oppression that in certain ways include me, but of which I may be unconscious, how can we retool perception or offer an oath to that so that people can raise themselves to that level of consciousness? That clicked in with some other reading that I've been doing. In the light of what we've been talking about, I've gone back to this book, *A Theology of Liberation*.[2]

JD: I'm just very slowly picking through this. I'm sure you're familiar with it. It's great. It's quite dense at times, so I'm reading a few pages and thinking about it, and I'm also using the index to dodge around. Someone else I've been thinking about is Herbert Marcuse. Gutierrez quotes Marcuse's 'Great Refusal' in *A Theology of Liberation*, this idea of the privileged becoming conscious and therefore taking the step of refusing all creature comforts, all modern conveniences, in the interests of levelling up across the board and bringing some more socio-economic equality and justice and therefore peace to everyone. I think this idea of the Great Refusal is very powerful, potentially, and I'm wondering if we need to bring that in. Then something that's been in my head whilst I've been starting to read Gutierrez. This Theology of Liberation, I'm trying to think about that as a White, middle-class man living in Britain right here, right now. Is there some space for something like a 'theology of solidarity'? That idea of solidarity is so key and that might be a way in for people.... We all need to be liberated, but [*he chuckles*] on another level, people may think in an objective way, 'What do *you* need to be liberated from?' I suppose it's intangibles, isn't it? I need to be liberated from my comfort, I suppose, amongst other things.

Finally, I happened across this book in an Oxfam bookshop before the lockdown started – *Arts Approaches to Conflict*.

NN: Oh, Liebmann. I've been at a workshop with Liebmann, yes.

JD: Fantastic. I saw this and thought, 'Let's have a look at this.' You'll know more about what Liebmann is up to than me. This is a collection of essays which she's edited. There are different essays on drama, visual arts, music, story-telling and combined arts, and different people are coming to this from their different perspectives, and asking how can they be used in processing and dealing with conflict. In the drama section there's an essay that's been put together by people who work with LEAP Confronting Conflict.[3] I was also interested in Belinda Hopkins' essay on Story-telling. It's interesting, on the first page of that, she refers to Kingston Friends Story-telling Group.... I suspect that that's a Quaker organisation. I wonder if this might feed into this idea, both our questions potentially, supporting the privileged in rising to consciousness of global and local economic systems, and how they hardwire privilege. It might then lead on in time to the voluntary embracing of Marcuse's Great Refusal. That's all bubbling away beside the fact that Friends in our Meeting are very excited and they said that we'll do an online discussion about this in early February. I'm thinking these ideas that you and I are knocking around now will hopefully fertilize what Charlie and I are going to do with that, and it might be a bit of a laboratory of these ideas. I don't know if any of that sparks thoughts.

NN: Yes... I think there are quite a number of strands that come to mind from your reflections on a number of issues sparked by the books and the thinking you've done. One of them is the silo-mentality.

Three Responses

NN: This is born from a tribal mentality. A categorization of 'them and us', 'in and out', and even in politics, when you heard Margaret Thatcher saying, 'He is not one of us'. 'He' was actually a Conservative! [*JD laughs.*] The person she is referring to is a Conservative, backed by a Conservative constituency, and had been there for years, but it's when you say, we have a new agenda and you're not coming on board.

You find it also in companies where production suffers because part of the organisation has adopted a silo-mentality and is holding back. It's when they cannot see the whole of the spectrum. They only see it fully from their perspective. They're ignoring the sum total of the reality, the context in which they work. Therefore, no matter how much good you do in your bit, it will always have minimal impact on the whole.

First of all, I believe that only those who are oppressed by their own privilege and therefore have a felt need to break out of their comfort zone, become allies. And that is the group we have talked about. This is the one-third. They are ready. They are not doing it for someone else. They are oppressed by their privilege, their class, their sexuality, oppressed by seeing the oppression of others. That is the group we start with.

The question is, how do we create a safe space for the second group who are *comme-ci-comme-ca*? They're not sure about coming in. If you don't have a lived experience that you want to break away from, that is where consciousness-raising comes in, and that's why I was very happy to have linked Nottingham Quaker Meeting with Nairobi Meeting in Kenya. They're starting to have a conversation. These two Quaker Meetings are, socially speaking, diametrically opposed. Whatever happens with those two groups, it's likely to divide people in the way we've been talking about.

So, a third will embrace, a third will find it difficult but possible, and a third will say, 'This is not what I want, this is not for me.' But they will have moved as a group, as a Meeting. So that bit where it's a lived experience of oppression of any kind, where you've come to the end of it and you've joined an AA meeting. If you have an alcohol problem, you seek therapy. You say, 'The status quo is too oppressive for me to continue as it is.' How do we create a safe space for those people to come?

And only those who live their lives or are beginning to live their lives inside-out, and for me inside-out living starts with saying, 'There but for the grace of God go I.'

This capacity for inspiring people is vital, because I am implicated. Therefore, being implicated, and my approach being informed by Gospel values, and as a Liberation Theology enthusiast, I make an option for the poor. This is where we come to my question: What's the best way of involving everyone to commit to 'speaking truth to power' in support of strengthening social cohesion?

We're speaking truth to power, if you take an option for the poor, it is imperative you have to speak truth to power. Now how you do it, and to what effect, from intent and impact? We have a lot of intentions of doing big good. Feeding the poor, ending poverty. All of those are good intentions. The impact of our intentions in my view is always undermined because we don't take in the strength of the enemy, the opposition. We're nice people, and we think we'll talk nicely to people, and they will nicely open the door. They don't see it that way. So for us, how do we not go as far as Camilo Torres? He said, 'I take off my cassock and take up my AK-47 to truly be a priest.' Now, I wouldn't go that far! Because what we are seeking is peaceful co-existence. So how do you seek that, taking an option for the poor, knowing that for the opposition... it is anathema to relinquish power. There has never been a relinquishing of power that we know of without people first trying to take it, whether it is slavery or women's votes, or Brixton riots, or Toxteth, all that. You don't have Lord Scarman coming to write a report until Brixton is burning.

Extending the Tent

NN: That is when the powerful who are threatened start saying, 'Let's find a middle ground.' So for me, it's knowing that we have in the Quaker community people going to the Occupy Movement who practise direct activism. Not everybody will do that, and therefore again it's having a spectrum from those who write a cheque to those who are at the forefront. Whatever we do in our conversation and our writing, how do we get a spectrum that allows people to find their comfort zone? The comfort zone is not one single zone, it is people finding it where a spectrum exists. A piece of ministry I once gave at Woodbrooke was about how our problem had to do with sexuality, in the widest context. I was saying, 'We have created a tent, where we are trying to do things that can only be done if the tent is extended. We need a bigger tent to include more people in order for the conversation that we want to happen.'

But when you have these 'big-small' tents which have already accommodated those who could be accommodated within the present context and agenda, others are still outside the tent, trying to be heard. They cannot be seen, they cannot be acknowledged, they are just voices. So how do we extend the tent? We extend the tent by doing what we are doing. Also, by running a reading group. If we start a reading group after this, we will first of all find people who are ready-made, in the first one-third. This linking of Meetings, conversations, like the one that your Meeting is having. It's about creating that safe space with other people... I believe very much in Matthew Fox's 'the original blessing'.[4] This 'original sin' concept has such a grip on us that we need to rework that theology for some people.

Coalitions

JD: You're absolutely right. I think that's one of the great Quaker revelations about original sin. Of course, there's sin in the world, we all have potential for sin. But that rejection of this notion of Augustinian original sin.... One time my wife, Monika, and I were visiting Oxford. We happened upon a small Orthodox church and got chatting with the priest, who was very keen when he realised that I was a Quaker, to talk about the connection between the two spiritual paths.

He said that Orthodox Christians are the same as Quakers theologically, they don't believe in original sin, they emphasise the resurrection of Christ and the fact that we're all saved. They're pan-sacramentalists. I wanted to bring in that idea that there are already lines of potential coalition, with apparently very powerful, very traditional, very good denominations. Other denominations like Orthodox Christianity might have no quarrel with us about that idea.

Enlarging the Tent

JD: That leads me onto something else. If we believe that we've been saved, and forgiven, again it's that question, 'What are you going to do about it?' It's wonderful that we're not labouring under that massive weight of original sin, we're not pulling that massive bundle of original sin around. That frees us, but to *do* something. *What* are we going to do with that potential, that possibility? Just to offer the image, the metaphor, of your image of the tent, and wanting to enlarge the tent. That made me think of the metaphor of lifting up the tent flaps so that you don't have that division at the sides, and the people standing just beyond the edge of your tent can be seen and heard more clearly, and maybe if they wish, they can step underneath the roof of the tent, once the flaps are up? [*They laugh.*]

What Do You Do with Your Baggage?

NN: Yes, yes, yes. I think... as Quakers what I have found even in doing 'Equipping for Ministry' and my Eva Koch Fellowship work at Woodbrooke, I *talk* to people, I approach people. We have one problem at Woodbrooke, though. I brought it out the last time I was at a tutors' conference, and that is, some of us have come to Quakerism with baggage, where we left somewhere else, not to come to Quakers necessarily, but because things were bad. It's like leaving a burning house. Then I was asking people, 'What about what you lost in that burning house? Was it that you left, then came and found this house of Quakers? Have you resolved those issues?' People are talking about the priest, the minister, 'I didn't like this, I didn't like what he did...' That was an opportunity that brought you here. You know, the *yin* and *yang*. Opportunity and crisis. That crisis gave you an opportunity to come here. There's nothing bad about that, but have you come to terms with that, because if you haven't you cannot live inside-out. It's almost a question of asking people, when you ask a man, 'When did you become a male Feminist? When did you become anti-racist?' There's a moment in time, just like a conversion. We turn around. That which has been naturally part of my upbringing, socialisation, in a negative sense, we turn around and say, 'No more!'

Now, there was one woman in that meeting, she took it very badly. Next morning, I sought her out and had breakfast with her and we ironed it out. She hadn't reconciled that, she still had baggage, from leaving the Anglican Church where she grew up, had been baptised, all that. We have to accept that there are 'walking wounded' Quakers, who are not ready to engage at this level of dialogue. The two words, Inclusion and Diversity, which means you have to give up some of your power and privilege. In order to do that, you have to be working from a healthy centre of being. It doesn't mean it is perfect, there is no perfection, but it's healthy enough to be able to recognise, 'This is my mess, and that is the mess out there.' The confidence is knowing that you and I are not so unique in what we are doing. There are people like us either doing it in isolation or in a community, or they don't know how to start. Once we go public, they will come. Like every movement, it starts small. Look at the anti-slavery Clapham Sect, just a small group – nearly fifty years later they were able to swing the vote in parliament.

Also, I have a lot of respect for the gay community. They have laboured and fought and found a position. Of course, there are differences, because there are White gay people who are in

Parliament, so they do have an advantage as strategists. They are very, very good. So, coming back to speaking truth to power. I'll say this and then give you a chance to respond. It's a spectrum, as I say. Write a cheque, demonstrate, write an article. Some people say, 'I'm into direct action.' Those people who are into direct action, they've committed themselves to that. But along this spectrum, everybody else is supporting every other person's attempt to live inside-out in the way they know. When Martin Luther King was killed, he was supporting dustbin collectors. That's where he had gone to show his solidarity. When a Nobel Peace Prize laureate walks alongside dustbin people, he could see, really *see*, everybody had a part to play on this spectrum.

A Spectrum of (Dis)comfort

JD: You know, that final remark you made about everyone having a part to play, maybe I'll start with this gut reaction.... I think that's absolutely right. I've scribbled down 'spectrum of (dis)comfort zones?' I like this idea, that there's a spectrum of experiences, of perspectives and responses, of zones where we feel comfortable, with the caveat that within that sense of being comfortable we've got to make space for being comfortable with some sense of discomfort. When you talk about our strategy, it strikes me that maybe that's where the strategy might be profitably and fruitfully applied. Identifying that spectrum, identifying how to create and facilitate that spectrum, and the connections between the zones and the people who will create that spectrum so it's not just disparate groups and individuals here and there doing things, and the left hand doesn't know what the right hand's doing, but they become aware of, and comfortable with, each other.

Amelia Lapeña-Bonifacio

JD: I like keeping an eye on Wikipedia (!) and I became aware of some people who passed away at the end of December.... I printed them off, because I found their stories so compelling. One is Amelia Lapeña-Bonifacio, who was a Filipino writer, academic, puppeteer, dramatist and so on.[5] She worked particularly in the medium of children's puppetry, but she wrote plays and short stories and whatnot. She was an academic for nearly forty years, but within that she also set up a children's puppet theatre. I can send you the article if you're interested.

NN: Yes, please.

JD: Within that she and her collaborators did satirical work, and worked very much with folk tales and folklore, within the Philippines and the East more generally, Indonesia and Japan and so on. They satirised the Marcos regime with a story they created about the Monkey King oppressing other animals and smashing them in order to have silence, and eventually smashing himself. They also worked with the victims of a volcanic eruption and presented puppet theatre work, having been encouraged to do so by doctors, as a means of helping the children to face that trauma, but also.... I remember as a kid I loved the film that Jim Henson made called *The Dark Crystal*, which is based around the ideas of *yin* and *yang*, the need for balance, reconciliation and peace.

It's really quite interesting; but I never knew that he made that film partly at least because Amelia Lapeña had criticised *Sesame Street*. She had said that she didn't think that *Sesame Street* would do very well in the East for three reasons. Firstly, there was a lot of play violence, and she was saying violence isn't the way, you're suggesting to children that it is, that doesn't work and it isn't helpful. Secondly, scenes in *Sesame Street* were short, and she was saying, if their attention spans are so short, why can kids in the Philippines deal with hour-long plays? And finally, there was a time when they played with food and threw it around. She said that didn't go down very well in the Developing World either. Whilst it might have been seen as comedy in the West, in the East whether or not you have enough food is a matter of life and death. Apparently, in response to her criticisms he went away and produced *The Dark Crystal*, which I think is great. He didn't try to just dismiss what she was saying, but thought about it and did something different, which is really good. I want to find out more about her, she sounds like an amazing person.

Jack Geiger

JD: What I've just said there might come back to what I was saying before about story-telling and the arts in approaching conflict? The other person I've heard about is H. Jack Geiger who was an American Jewish doctor and a pioneer of Social Medicine,[6] which is basically a term for doctors addressing the contextual and social reasons for illness and sickness, as well as the medical side of things. He sounds amazing, his father was a doctor, his mother was a microbiologist. They had left Germany and Austria respectively. He was raised in New York, there was a whole stream of family members who were escaping from the Nazis through the 1930s, he was born in 1925, so he heard their stories.

Very precocious, graduated high school at 14, was too young to go straight to university, got a job as a copy boy on the *New York Times*. He started to hang out in Jazz clubs. His parents weren't that pleased about that.... But through that he made friends with a Black actor called Canada Lee, who he'd met backstage after a performance of *Native Son*, then Lee agreed with Geiger's parents that he would take him in, so he left.... He'd run away from home previously, I think, but reconciled with his parents and they agreed that Lee would act as a father figure to him, and then for about a year he was living with Lee, which brought him into contact with all these really interesting artistic people: Richard Wright, Paul Robeson, Orson Welles.... Then at fifteen, Lee advances him a loan that allows him to go off to university for the first time....

He became a journalist, he served in the Second World War, joining the Merchant Marine specifically because it was the only branch of the armed forces that was fully-integrated at that time, and he served under the only Black Merchant Marine captain in the Second World War. He then starts pre-med studies, but because he's demonstrating so much against racism, he's blackballed and can't get a medical degree, so he becomes a science journalist instead. Later, through his journalism he's taken on to study medicine, the way opens and he becomes involved in Social Medicine, challenging land mines and nuclear war. He's involved in two organisations that are awarded the Nobel Peace Prize, and a whole load of other public health awards. Covered in glory.

NN: Wow, that's amazing.

JD: He writes this book called *The Doctor-Activist*. It's all about being involved in the context, helping the whole person. I can send you the article.... I don't believe he was a Quaker but there's so much that's admirable that Quakers could respond to and maybe draw something from.

None of These Diseases

NN: Yes. By the way, have you come across a book, it's a very old book, *None of these Diseases*.

JD: No, I don't think so, no.

NN: A medic looked at the Old Testament laws, dietary, medical and so on, and he showed that you wouldn't get these diseases if you followed that. I read it, thirty, forty years ago. As you were talking that came to mind. I'll try and look it up for myself and again.... There are inspirational individuals, where we can spark ideas from. I took a Japanese puppeteer to Kenya with her Irish husband to do story-telling.... All these interesting people, they have a story to tell, but they also have a lesson to teach. I always find there's a lesson I can glean from this rich tapestry of a person's life that's interesting. The other thing as you were talking that came to mind was just how much a small organisation, the Quakers, has accomplished. Sometimes we don't give it enough credence.

Tonight, I'm hoping to have a Zoom meeting with the European section of FWCC. I'm looking forward to getting to know them. But in looking at who we've been, where we've been over the years, the *impact* on both our context and on us. We had intention and then we had impact, which is admirable to see, but it seems to me that it is those 'historical good marks', if you will, that attract a lot of people. And it's how we now create our own reality for the future generations. One of the things we haven't talked about, you and I, is how do we begin serious interactions with Young Quakers?

Reaching Out to Other Groups

NN: How do we, you and I, make ourselves credible to these young people with an agenda and approach and outlook? They're a force of nature in the widest sense [*they both laugh*].

JD: Yes, absolutely.

NN: They need to be given more credence than they currently have and I remember being given a six-month contract by Lambeth Council. It was to get six youth organisations in the borough which were run by these old men and one or two women, but no young people, and my task was to work with them, show them how they could re-write their constitutions, how they could learn, because when young people had come on the boards, the older members had pulled rank and the young people had left…. Well-meaning and good people unknowingly pull rank, and then they say, 'What did we do that they left?' It's because they hadn't taken into account, if young people come on the board, they have to change. It can't be business as usual, because that was what they wanted to do. If you have women on the board, if you have Black people on the board, it cannot be business as usual.

How do you help change perceptions? You change perspectives, you change the narrative. Some people have only one narrative, you wheel it around everywhere you go, and [*he laughs*] you feel very uncomfortable about changing it, so in our discussion we've still got to think about how we can do that. Last year in the summer, I wrote that article about theology for young people for the American magazine *Friends Journal*... in a postmodern society, theology has to be, not repackaged exactly, but you've got to take it apart. If you try to repackage in a new container without taking it apart, you're going to have alien elements in it. And those are the alien elements keeping young people, Black people away. It seems to me that we need to find a new way of including young people – and everybody else! It's about theo-praxis.[7] Good. I think we're soon coming to the end of the hour...

6: Practising Freedom: Moving Along the Path of Continuing Revelation
13 January, 2021

Nim's discussion point:

- As our Quaker understanding of our testimonies informs our spirituality in engaging with corporate, individual and societal relationships, how do we translate 'that of God in everyone' in a socially manifest way?

Jonathan's discussion point:

- How does the notion of holisticity relate to the way in which religion can harden prejudice, simplify/make literal the complex and metaphorical, and how certain types of religious faith can encourage an 'us and them' attitude? Equally, how can religion be an engine of positive change across societies, cultures and the world?

Upcoming Projects...

We started with some small talk; Jonathan talked about his impending move to Nottingham....

JD: Anyway, how are things at your end?

NN: Oh, quiet really... not much happening on this side, I take it easy, I have a rhythm of life I adopt.... I'm just preparing for our Area Meeting. I'm doing a session on becoming a Quaker Diversity and Inclusion Ally, a short presentation and a little workshop, which was postponed from last year. I also picked up... there's a woman called Liz Oppenheimer. She had some sort of Damascus Road experience and became a Diversity Ally, so that's the one I want people to consider.

Thank you for the information about Jack Geiger and Amelia Lapeña. I'll look at that, but a quick glance told me that they will be interesting. Now, today, we're on the sixth question....

So for me, it's interesting, because they seem to dovetail a little, your sixth and my sixth: 'As our Quaker understanding of our testimonies inform our spirituality in engaging with corporate, individual and societal relationships, how do we translate "that of God in everyone" in a socially manifest way?'

JD: I thought the same thing… would you like to kick off this time?

'Can Anything Good Come Out of Nazareth?'

NN: Yes… I think for me, quite interestingly there is that biblical question that was asked, 'Can anything good come out of Nazareth?' That was asked of Jesus Christ. [*He chuckles.*] This backwards place that had no significance, and then you think what exactly is the yardstick, what is your point of reference, what are you taking into account, to come to that conclusion that makes you ask that question, because, it's a very dismissive question. It's almost saying, 'I know the area. I know the people. I know the conditions. I know the reality of the area is that nothing good could come out of there. It's a no-go area.'

Audre Lorde

NN: For me that is really the basis for the whole thing about the unconscious bias, and I don't see us being able to move forward until two things occur: firstly, becoming aware, and even before that, accepting the concept of unconscious bias, becoming aware of what unconscious bias is and how it dictates our thoughts, ideas, feelings, outlook, perceptions, perspectives, conclusions, frames of reference, all that. The other thing is, you know what Audre Lorde said, that the master's tools will never dismantle the master's house. She was saying, some want to work with us without doing the hard work of being able to identify what kind of tools they have been bequeathed that allowed them to build their world view, their comfort zone. They're the same tools that they use to maintain their privileged positions, their comfort zones, and there is no way forward if they're proposing to use the same tools to dismantle that comfort zone.

In order to dismantle the comfort zone, to move beyond that privilege, we need another set of tools. We need to believe that the tools you have serve a purpose up to a point, but that's not the whole story. They serve a purpose, *served* a purpose. But in serving that purpose, they have also excluded other people because those tools cannot serve the purpose of the excluded. In fact, when I was thinking about that, what came to mind is your picture of not just extending the tent, but removing the flaps so people can talk, which at one level, it's an admirable picture, and effective, until I thought of *rain*! [*They laugh.*] The people in the tent are privileged. The elements will not touch them, and although they have extended the range of engagement they're saying, 'We don't just own this space for ourselves, and in order to be inclusive, I need to see you, and you need to see me.' That's why the flaps are removed. But it's still a very comfortable zone you're in. That doesn't mean that that is wrong, because it's what I call 'kind intention'. Those kind intentions begin with a person saying, 'I will stay in the tent. I will remove the flaps, and I will talk to you, engage with you from here.' What you haven't asked me is, 'Do you want to come into the tent?!' [*They laugh.*] Do we want to enlarge the tent, or do we all want to *leave* the tent?

JD: I was just thinking that, yes, maybe the tent needs to disappear entirely.

The Books on Your Shelf

NN: Yes. Therefore, it's almost saying that good, kind intentions, without changing the impact, just remain good intentions. There's a lot of that with some of the people I've read, some Quakers, well-meaning Quakers, there is almost intellectual timidity. They are timid. I don't totally discard timidity as a starting point, because when you put your toe into the water before you jump into the river, that's alright [*he laughs*] because you are *testing* the water. Timidity in terms of testing is fine. You don't jump into the deep end and end up getting drowned, because that is about reflecting. You *reflect*. It's a good starting point.

So having reflected, taken into account, and acquired the right reading of the situation, then you need to put timidity aside and start engaging fully. Now, without going through a process of unconscious bias training of some sort, whether individually or with others, where you begin to see things in a more balanced fashion, that will remain a great challenge. Because, for me, the underlying thing is, we don't see the world as it is, we see it *as we are*. Therefore when we're saying we've got to see and engage with an alternative reality, that has not been part of your socio-political, economic, spiritual journey. That's reflected in the books you have on your shelf, the music you listen to, the people you hang around with, the papers you read. There is that dimension that means all that reality has bequeathed you a world view, if you want the tools to engage. If we are saying that there is another *dimension* of reality that we are seeking, that's very interesting. I was just looking again at the Yearly Meeting 2017; you know that minute?

JD: Yes.

NN: It says, 'We have had the call to examine our own diversity, particularly in our committee and organisational structure, locally and nationally. Diversity has several key dimensions.... We ask Meeting for Sufferings to look at how we can remove barriers and actively seek wider participation in the wider life of our Meetings, paying particular attention to race and age diversity and to keep Yearly Meeting informed in their annual report.' So that commitment is there, and therefore it is a matter of the practice. How do we turn that into reality for those good intentions to have an impact? That is the challenge as I see it.

JD: All of that I recognise and respond to. As you were talking, I was thinking... [*he chuckles*] well my first thought was that I need to read more Audre Lorde, because I think she's on the money. But I was also thinking, I had the phrase, 'continuing revelation'. In a sense, Quaker commitment to continuing revelation offers us a path, a blueprint, a roadmap for doing this, bearing in mind and having to accept that even though continuing revelation is such a precious and valued part of Quaker theology and history, actually a lot of the time, it's something that there's the potential for us to say, 'We *believe* in continuing revelation.' And we have received all these fruits of continuing revelation, but just like all those people before us who we might consider and think, 'Ah, they allowed that to concretise, they allowed their insights to become ossified and fixed in stone, and now they're too rigid, they're not liberal and free-minded like us.' We have that potential danger as well.

Be Comfortable with Discomfort

JD: Because there's a difference between valuing the continuing revelation that's brought us to where we are, the Society where we personally feel comfortable and welcome and happy in, and continuing to apply that continuing revelation to ourselves and everything else, that links back to that idea of getting comfortable with discomfort.

I think that there's that need, and that's challenging, and I think that's one thought I'll be offering to Quakers in Yorkshire when Charlie and I do our presentation. Knitted in with that is Paulo Freire's use of the term 'praxis', that idea of analysis, discussion and pedagogy, but also being and doing and applying the insights you gain from education as the practice of freedom. I've just been dipping into bell hooks' book *Teaching to Transgress* which is a revelation to me and I love the idea that she's responding to Freire. There's a chapter on him. She uses several interesting terms, such as 'engaged pedagogy' and another is 'liberatory pedagogy'. I like that idea of engagement, that speaks strongly in me to my interest in Dialogism and Bakhtin's idea of the Dialogical, and the need for contact and connection and engagement between different people and things. The Self and the Other have to come into contact and interact in order to fully be themselves. Bakhtin has this quote, I'm quoting off the top of my head, 'My search for a self takes the form of a quest: I go out to the other in order to come back with a self.'

NN: No, that is the concept of *Ubuntu*, the South African *Ubuntu*, very much the same.

JD: Okay. You are only truly yourself when you're in contact with others, and that leads me to something that's becoming a bit of a mantra: the Self needs the Other. White need Black, Black need White. Young need Old. Able-bodied need disabled, Gay need straight.... And so on, *vice versa*, we all need the Other, like it or not [*he laughs*] and we won't always like that, and it won't always be easy, but we all need the Other in order to truly be ourselves. That's my instinctive response to your question and I think it also links in with my question.

It's the third part of my question about holisticity: how do we deal with the way in which religion can harden prejudice, simplify and/or make literal the complex and metaphysical, and how certain types of religious faith can encourage an 'Us and them' attitude? Equally, how can religion become an engine of positive change across societies, cultures, and the world? It's a more religiously inflected version of your question, I think. That's how can we craft a praxis based on those hopefully Quakerly insights that are useful for Quakers and hopefully useful for non-Quakers as well. How can we craft a model of that praxis which isn't going to be off-putting to people who are lukewarm about religion, but offering insights which are universalised for everybody?

Resolutions That Keep Us at It

NN: As you were talking, what came to mind was how millions of people around the world, with all good intentions and commitment, start their New Year's resolutions. [*They both laugh.*]

JD: Yeah. Me included.

NN: For most of them by the end of January, it's lying on the wayside. Now, you can't fault them on the good intentions but, if you ask, 'Did you just wake up one morning saying what my resolution will be?' – No! I thought about it, I'd taken some things into account and said, 'A better me will emerge, better in whatever way, and I believe the vehicle to deliver this better me is this resolution that I make.' This is what I say about good intentions, kind intentions, nobody has imposed them on you. You've come up with them for your own benefit, you've actually published them, announced them to folk: 'This is what I want to do.' So what has happened with the motivation to keep on keeping on?

I tend to think if you have a group of people, who have ditched their New Year's resolutions, we're going to examine *why*, what happened. How do you come up with New Year's resolutions that *keep you at it*? How do you understand that any objective has obstacles, and how do you overcome obstacles to meet your objectives? Your objectives are alright, you just hadn't taken in the nature of the obstacles, i.e., the strength of the enemy, if you want. We don't fail you on the objective and the intention. It's just that you had not taken into account other things like the nature of the obstacles. That's when you say, can we come together, we who have ditched our resolutions and yet we still believe in this commitment? Getting comfortable with discomfort – why? Why should I do that? For what purpose? How strong am I to actually cope with discomfort without being dismantled by it, so to speak?

When you said to me, which makes a lot of sense and is quite understandable, when you went to Kenya, to Nairobi, and you saw what was happening with poverty, you came back and said, 'Part of my discomfort will be to drink less coffee, something I like, something I choose, something I can afford.' Nobody's telling me not to do it, I tell myself not to do it. Why? Nobody's watching me, I choose. Why do you choose? Where does the motivation come from? There's nothing wrong with New Year's resolutions or good intentions when they support what you're trying to do. How do we keep the course, how do we keep going? Part of that is, of course, finding like-minded people, who keep reminding us.

That's why I have the greatest respect for AA meetings. A group of people that surpasses culture, it works in all cultures, for men, for women, in South Africa, in Nevada, anywhere. This set of principles people adhere to in a group, in a meeting place, where your needs are met and you *believe* in it. You're not forced to do it. For me, it's how do we create that kind of environment where we say those people whose New Year's resolutions are okay can meet with people whose New Year's resolutions are *not* okay [*they laugh*] and we can both have a dialogue, because it's about building relationships, and these resolutions were to meet specific needs, so they were larger than us. Where is the motivation? Where is the stickability? How do you stick with it?

No Pain, No Gain

JD: As you were talking, two things were in my mind. My initial response was to relate it back to myself. When I make a resolution, sometimes they stick and other times not – why *is* that? One thought was, when people want to get fit, you hear that slogan, 'No pain, no gain,' so, certainly, in the physical realm, but also in other, emotional, moral realms as well, sometimes that message is another way of saying you need to get comfortable with discomfort, but there are benefits of one kind or another. Health benefits, mental, physical health benefits, moral benefits, whatever. So that's one thing – no pain, no gain.

But again, there's that little voice at my shoulder saying that that sometimes works, but it doesn't always work. Still, it would bear some thinking about, why it sometimes works and sometimes doesn't, because 'No pain, no gain' is true all the time, and people know it's true. Also, my point from a previous conversation was also chiming: if we can somehow plait together this idea of being comfortable with discomfort, no pain no gain, but also when it's possible, locating the pleasurable sides of the praxis, the fact that it isn't all very admirable, noble, painful good work, but actually a lot of it can bring benefits that are enjoyable and comfortable in a sense. So when you're talking about groups of like-minded people who are sympathetic to each other, be that AA or a discussion group of another type, but there you have the potential for friendship and acquaintanceship and community and so on, which people enjoy, just getting together with each other and discussing things and hearing about other people's lives, that's pleasant and enjoyable. That's one of the reasons why we do it, as well as what we learn through doing it. So one thing, once we've completed this conversation period and process, maybe one of the challenges we're setting for ourselves is to come up with definite suggestions for how the praxis can be put into action, and also reasons that can be offered for why people should be thinking seriously about the praxis.

NN: I totally agree. For me one of the greatest statements encouraging us humans to grow spiritually is when Jesus said, 'Only those who hunger and thirst after righteous shall be filled.' Where you are painfully aware of your own deficiency of food and water just as you're aware of your deficiency of your righteousness, and you hunger for it to that extent – you will be filled with it. That's the promise. The topic we have, we have spiritual promises, psychological promises, theological promises, which we organise under the heading of 'social justice', and that to me means that you cannot live in isolation in a multi-racial, multi-cultural, multi-faith, non-faith world. We cannot live well with the tools with which we're already living. We need to get that right – expressing to each other our understanding that we are painfully aware of our deficiencies, but how do we put that in a way that people say, 'There is a hunger for righteousness to be filled'? Just as someone is aware of their alcoholism, then they find a group of people, in a programme. It has been tested and it has worked. That's what they commit to.

JD: It's interesting, I'm not sure if this is globally the case, but certainly in America, AA has religious status, because they accept a power beyond themselves... I'm not totally familiar with their whole plan, but that's certainly one of their requirements. I'm just aware that for us, there is a religious-spiritual aspect to all of this that we are unembarrassed about discussing.

Reconciling Different Positions

JD: I'm also aware that, for us, God, however we understand 'God', that divine force wants this to happen. I'm also aware that lots of other people out there, of different religious groups and affiliations, might use different language, but largely they agree with us, we're reading off the same hymn sheet, and that's fine. But I'm also aware that there are lots of people who consider themselves not to be religious, who are very proud of the fact that for them there isn't that spiritual dimension, and yet they may very well embrace this project, or they may be in the second one-third who potentially will embrace this project. I'm just wondering if we also need at some stage to consider that gap between our language and culture as religious people in the broadest sense, and people who are Humanists or whatever, who may want to work with us on that, yet that spiritual aspect of it doesn't work for them. We need to think about how we reconcile those positions.

Love Is... love

NN: Yes. I think on that point, two quick things. In what we are trying to do with Quakers, we have been initiated into doing this, so we don't need another initiation. It's just how to go forward. On the other question, there is nothing that says, 'I love my wife in a Christian way. I love my wife in a Muslim way. I love my wife and children in a Buddhist way....' Love! There is something we understand wherever you come from, whether you believe in God or not. There is no, 'I love my wife as an Atheist' (!) [*They laugh.*] What we have to know, there is an overarching language and a way of framing what we're doing that says that this is a Human enterprise. It is bequeathed to humanity. Now, how do we universalise it, knowing that we can bring it to Quakers, but also take it out in a universal way?

7: How Do You Read *Animal Farm*? Different Responses to the Challenges Facing Us 20 January, 2021

Nim's discussion point:

- Quakers have developed a certain spiritual pride believing we are good people with a good record of social justice and pointing to certain admirable achievements. How effectively do we move from 'resting on our laurels'?

Jonathan's discussion point:

- Again, working with 'holisticity'...
  - ○ Culture/media: again, how can these factors reflect certain other factors — either positively or negatively?

Getting Going

We started discussing general news, and then Nim began to talk about a session on race and racism that he had run for his Quaker Area Meeting.

NN: I'd given them a small article about this White Quaker who'd had a breakthrough in terms of coming to terms with racism and her Quakerism.

JD: Is this Liz Oppenheimer?[1]

NN: Yes. We went into smaller groups. All I wanted was for them to come up with one insight from that story, come up with one action they were going to take, either individually or as a Meeting, and come up with one question that we could pursue, because we had only one hour. We've done some notes to send to everybody, and I was saying a stand-alone activity does not solve anything. It's a taster, it's a bite-size thing. [*They both chuckle.*] That's all it is. But somebody sent me a card saying they'd also bought the book I had recommended about Black Presence, which they are reading. My Meeting has asked me to do a second stage, take it further, so I think it's just a matter of being able to engage from where we're at. There's a continuum, and the moment you get on the continuum, the journey has started. That's why it is not a one-time activity, you've got to walk the continuum. So, we are on Question 7, are we?

JD: I believe so, yes.

NN: Do you want to begin today?

JD: Okay. My question is the final sub-division of my fourth question, about the notion of 'holisticity', both in terms of how negative factors are intimately bound up within the weave of our lives and so are difficult to unravel, but also the importance of taking a holistic approach to weaving in positive changes and attitudes within our everyday lives. Then part (d) of the question is about culture and media: how can these factors reflect, magnify, and/or engender certain factors, attitudes, and forces – either positively or negatively? At this point, obviously, I was sitting and generating different ideas.... This was me riffing on the topic and I was thinking about how things are hardwired or made to appear hardwired to reinforce privilege for certain categories of people in certain contexts.

In this environment, we're talking about massive White privilege. I was writing this comment down from the point of view of all the different economic, social, political factors that are reinforcing White privilege and making it seem inevitable, and justifying it. Also perhaps reacting against any challenge to that privilege. So, I'm just going to go with it... I'm thinking about all the ways in which culture and media take it for granted in the British context that the White context is the dominant one, and that that is right and good. Certainly, that's been the prevailing attitude up until a few years ago, it's very slowly starting to shift. The obvious ways that it's started to shift, you're seeing more non-White actors now, in the media, dramas and so forth. That's certainly happened through my lifetime; I've become aware of that happening more and more, which is a good thing. I think there are places and contexts where we can see the whole issue of White privilege starting to be inspected and discussed at different levels. That's a good thing.

A Timely Challenge

JD: You also still see, I think, people offering some kind of push-back, some kind of challenge to any kind of radical question of privilege. That can take different forms. At the start of the Covid crisis. I didn't follow it up that far, but I saw that in some newspapers there were opinion piece writers who were saying, 'The Covid Crisis is a necessary challenge to the Woke Generation!' [*They both laugh.*] My understanding was, there's a certain type of conservative, probably White, fairly privileged themselves, very traditional in their attitudes, who's very fond of saying things like, 'What we need is a War. What we need is a proper crisis.'

'World War Two made young men grow up and get out there, and think about other people, and sacrifice things,' as if the Woke generation aren't thinking about others and sacrificing things. I think this remark about Covid being a timely challenge to the Woke Generation is saying something similar, that the Woke Generation somehow is self-indulgent, they're wanting to stir things up for the hell of it, they're superficial, they don't want to understand the way things are, or they wouldn't be challenging it.

It made me cross, really. Covid is a timely challenge for everybody. So I'm bringing that in, I'm bringing in the Occupy Movement – I have very vivid memories of David Cameron going out of his way to try to suggest that people involved in that movement were criminal, habitual drug users. He dropped that into speeches at some point, suggesting if you went down there, all you'd smell was cannabis smoke. Monika, my wife, and I visited one of the Occupy places, and we did smell some cannabis smoke – but does that mean that everyone in the

Occupy Movement was a cannabis user? No, it doesn't mean that at all. So there's all of that and I'm aware that even though society is moving in a positive direction incrementally, you've got to continue in that direction.

There's a Chinese saying about learning. It's a case of swimming up-river all the time. If you stop swimming, you'll move backwards.

It's the same with any kind of gains for any group of people whatsoever, and what you have to do is keep going... I was going to mention Trump.... Look at the way he tried to criminalise the Black Lives Matter Movement, whilst he constantly tried to let off the White Militias who were doing far worse things. But actually, let's be fair. Look at Boris Johnson, who's written blatantly racist things in journalism, and it has been laughed off by so many people and he went on to be elected Prime Minister of this country.

The British Situation

JD: It's not fair to just point at America. It's happening here in Britain as well. It's just that, overall, British people tend to be a little more muted and quote 'polite', but it's all there, the racism, the traditionalism and the conservatism are all still there, because people who like Boris Johnson will still tell me, 'Oh well, he's witty, he's charming, he gets the job done. You know, he's gaffe-prone, but he doesn't really mean it.' And I'm thinking, 'No, he *did* mean it when he wrote those statements, with those racist statements which we're both familiar with so I won't repeat them here, and he knew that it would have a certain effect and that it was going to reinforce a particular voter base for him.'

So, talking through that, then, as someone who's an English teacher, I'm into reading, I write things as well, my response is, 'Right, how do I engage with that in a positive and constructive way?' I think that it takes various forms, as most things do. I've got to read critically and I've got to challenge things where I feel that they are inappropriate or wrong. But in a systematic, thoughtful way, persuasively. That's one thing. I've got to ask myself, whenever I feel moved to write. When I'm writing something, is this a moment when I need to be dealing with these issues? I may not always be moved to write about this particular issue, and there will be times when I am challenged to write about it. I've got to make sure that I don't evade it, because it might be uncomfortable for me, but I've got to bring my critical-creative faculties to bear on it. Also, like we've said previously, it's about unearthing those buried, hidden histories and gems and stories that have been silenced.

Helen Morgan Brooks

JD: I keep thinking about Helen Morgan Brooks.... My instinct is telling me, I've got to check and see what's out there on her. I suspect there's not a huge amount. There's this very good section in *Black Fire*, and there are a couple of obituaries that were published at the time of her death, there's some of her own writing in Quaker magazines as well as the poetry. I need to check all that. I need to see if there's something that I can write about her life and work. So those are my three positive offerings around this issue.

'New Racism'

NN: Yes, I see. I think because what we are tackling is so wide, so deep, so big, so entrenched, we need multiple approaches... as I was reminding the group I worked with on Sunday, I came to think about it later more deeply: good intentions, implementation, impact. It's in that way where we are both asking ourselves: are we talking about personal, systemic, organisational, culture? Because for some of us, we have to start with the personal, and then widen that circle out to the people who we can influence. One thing you mentioned that was very critical and very true, is what is called 'New Racism'. It's almost a decline in the social acceptability of extreme racism. We know it's still underlying there because again and again you hear people apologising for having been caught out with racist remarks, when they thought the camera wasn't switched on, the microphone was off, and yet, 'Deep down, I'm not racist, I don't believe that, this was a one-off.' In a way it's progress, but it can sideline us when we think that now we know that there are things that are not socially acceptable that are being dropped in the public sphere. Those are the people who clothe themselves in expediency, religious expediency, whatever expediency you wish. Like with Black Lives Matter, there were a lot of companies that came out saying, 'We support this!' Even that American coffee shop that was caught out with racism, what do they call it?

JD: Starbucks?

NN: Yes, Starbucks. Part of their response was to close their world-wide business for an *afternoon* for a workshop [*he chuckles*] on racism. So, the notion of tokenism, which is a child of New Racism, is sometimes helped by 'opinion gathering', which is just like grafting. I have a worker in Kenya who likes grafting things on trees and things [*he laughs*] and they look good! But they are *grafted* to something else. They don't have deep roots into the soil, and therefore with this whole thing, people can *graft*, they can opinion-collect, they can gather information like Starbucks, and say, 'We've done our bit.' This is why, even with us as Quakers I keep saying a one-off weekend or session, these are just tasters and they should compel us to move further, but I'm also equally clear that there is a spiritual dimension to all this. There have always been people who are counter-cultural, throughout history. They did not go with the mainstream. They did not have to belong to the tribe, they did not have to belong to their class, they were not enslaved. They were free people. They were men who fought alongside women, Whites who fought alongside Blacks, so there is always a people, a mind-set that is able to read reality and say, 'I am on this side.' That is where I get a lot of my hope.

Where are we going to locate our centre of operations? Is it in academia? Is it as practitioners? Is it as activists? Can we do all three? How do we play to our strengths? Now, I don't think many people, especially Quakers, would disagree about the good intentions of the BYM 2017 minute. The issue we disagree about is implementation. You'll remember that I mentioned a Quaker Meeting where they said they were for the environment, but not for Black Lives Matter.

Building a Critical Mass

NN: So, implementation and what constitutes impact – personal, in our Meeting, societal, and so on, is a key consideration. The big issue for me with impact is resources. Quakers have always funded piecemeal the Black workers post until this time. Now they've made it a permanent post. The impact we're considering is, even with government policy, if it's under-resourced, it won't happen. Therefore, this bit where we're talking at different levels, there'll be activists talking about resources, academics who'll be writing books and delivering workshops, and practitioners who are doing what you were doing at the weekend and what I was doing at the weekend. So we can all support people who are playing to their strengths. If your strength is towards the academic, you can support the others. But – how to build a critical mass that speaks, and things move?

We've had two women prime ministers, so we could say, 'Oh, we're doing very well.' We've had one Black president: 'Oh, Blacks are doing very well!' This symbolic manifestation of the issues, we shouldn't give them more credence than they are due. Thatcher never appointed any women to the Cabinet, apart from Baroness Young in the early Eighties. She had her own agenda.

How do *we* build a critical mass within *our* movement? The other thing, is not to be naïve. Most people relinquish power reluctantly. Most people want to hold onto their position. Remember there are, what, seven types of power: personal, positional, resource, coercive, expert, referent and connection. All these types of power, if you look in our society, they are all held by White men. Not even White women, White *men*. To relinquish it is very difficult, until you're implicated if you don't relinquish it. That is why MacMillan could tell the South African parliament, 'The winds of change! They're coming! You can do absolutely nothing about that.' It's knowing you'd better jump off the ship before *you* are sunk, not the ship sinks! [*They laugh.*] For Quakers, I think when we come to write, soon I hope, all of our articles, I don't know how we can couch it, where we put the message through that lies about racism are done with words and also with *silence*. You can't just be non-racist. That is the silent bit. Being anti-racist is where you are saying, I will confront. Non-racist people are just colour blind. As I asked a group at Woodbrooke once, 'If you are colour blind, how come you can see the colours of the rainbow and the colours of our flag?' So that's where I think. Again, going back to what we have said, which I totally believe, you and I and others constitute the one-third that are not silent. We also know others who are silent but want to not be silent anymore. Then there is the other third who we know are not ready.

Silences, William Penn and Animal Farm

JD: Your point about silence potentially links, perhaps ironically, with Quaker silence, the fact that there are different qualities of silence. Some are good, others are neutral, others are negative, and it's a potential criticism that Quakers are open to a silence that can be used to cover as much as to give space to the revelation of things. That sent me back to thinking about Quaker narratives and how vital it is, not to dish the dirt for the sake of it, I mean we're all clear that William Penn did a lot of great things, but there's this other part to the story, and if you're going to understand him as a human being, you've got to understand that he wasn't perfect. He did do things that we lament. Actually, if you look at the record, I think there were moments when he was aware that he was doing things that were wrong as well, but he didn't actually go the whole way to admitting it. I think honestly confronting the whole truth is a big part of it. I wonder if there'll be some push-back from some parts of the Religious Society of Friends about that? Not universally, but I wonder if some people will push back against that.

NN: When you say, 'against that' which part do you mean?

JD: Against efforts to bring up and reveal those hidden bits of history, for instance that William Penn owned slaves, which personally I wouldn't be surprised if the majority of Quakers don't realise. It could well come as a surprise. I might be completely wrong, but then in actually being faced with that, because he's such a respected Quaker figure, I wonder if some people might want to react against that, and it's finding a way of presenting it so that people can take it on and deal with it, rather than just wanting to deny it, avoid it, or minimise it.

NN: Yes… there's something I call the *Animal Farm* mentality. [*He laughs.*] There are some people who say, 'Look, I'm not interested in anything other than this story of these animals who kick out this farmer and take over. I don't want to read anything else into it, so don't bring politics into it!' [*They laugh.*] When we really accept the continuum, in one sense you're saying, from a novice to an expert, or an activist, you are engaging with issues in the public arena, through direct action. On this continuum, people who are at each end, unless you are well-centred, you who are at this end will be nasty to the person at the other end. Or you may think that where they are is of no importance, and this person may say the same. 'I just want to hear the good bits about Quaker history!' As I was saying to someone else, it's the other side of the coin. It's as Jesus says, 'Whose head is on the coin? Caesar's!' Having committed ourselves is knowing that there are people we can almost predict will have issues with this.

'When They Go Low, We Go High.'

If we oppose the master, in any religion... there is no religious leader who has never been opposed, it's how we are centred so that being generous in spirit, we will speak truth to power, wherever that power might reside and do what Michelle Obama says, 'When they go low, we go high.' I'm not going down to their level! I'm not going down to that level of circular conversation, I will not respond to that, I do not belong there. I don't want to talk about that. That's what I was saying about playing to our strengths. I would rather convince a policy maker, a decision maker, and would put more of my effort there. Because it needs just one such change to take a step forward.

The day after the Race Relations Act came into effect, nobody had any posters that read, 'No Blacks, no dogs, no Irish.' They were all removed. You could have talked to those hoteliers for yonks, and one of the people who did that was Michael Heseltine. His autobiography is very interesting. He ran a hotel. In the early days he sent a Ghanaian couple to his friend's hotel. He had rung his friend and asked, 'Do you have a vacancy, because I don't have vacancies for here tonight.' And the friend had said, 'Yes, send them over.' He sent them over. They came back. On their way back, he called Heseltine: 'Why did you send them to *me*? Why would you think I would allow them to be in my hotel?' They had never talked about the race issue, so he hadn't known this guy's views. I remember reading that and thinking, 'Yeah, I don't agree with most of your politics, but I do agree with some of the things you say.' [*He chuckles.*] One of the things, for me, is the time factor. If we want to see an impact, what is it that we pick up first? That's why I was saying, for me in the end, what I see is articles, a reading list of books to recommend, as a starting point, and doing what we are doing. You are doing that, I am doing this, talking to people, and that's the starting point. But we can still have a group of non-book club people, because if you are saying, academics, practitioners, activists, at what level do you pitch the discussion?

Effective Questions to Ask

JD: Okay. Can I put something in here? Just ask a question, really. Alongside all of that I'm wondering, might it be a good idea to think of practical suggestions for different ways into dealing with the issues? Also, I'm aware that I took Linda Murgatroyd's three questions about dealing with Climate Change[2] and developed them a little but in terms of race and racism. I really liked what you did with your workshop on Sunday, one insight, one action, one question; and I'm wondering if there might be some scope as well, maybe as an appendix to what we write, maybe a resource bank at the end. Suggested questions and tools and activities. What do you think?

A Possible Way Forward

NN: I was actually thinking more in terms of an appendix which would be a ten-hour model. One-hour sessions, ten weeks. Then people can choose, because if we organise all of this, when we come to unpack the transcript, we'll find out.... Here we have a novice and an activist in a non-challenging setting. How do we start, because part of it, it's a journey, a journeying into self. I've got things I've done in the past which I can share. So something like that where we are saying, this is how to start. You can do it individually, with a partner, or as a group. With these questions, just one hour, for ten weeks. A quarter of that is consciousness-raising; a quarter is information giving, which you have to grapple with; another quarter is where you are almost inducted, and the final quarter is where you are now ready for the next phase, whether to ask more questions, read more, join a group, to start being an activist of sorts, or to commit yourself to offering these ten hours to another group. Or to rewrite it in a way that makes sense to you.[3]

All we're saying is, please tell us how you use it, so we can update it. So it's an ongoing thing. We're also saying, these good intentions – what do we do with them? I think it's what you alluded to earlier. We can't always take into account the strength of your position; it could be the strength of your feelings. People may have feelings that are so strong, but they are not ready to engage with this material.... Mannenheit said about Friends developing a certain pride, and in my final question, I think what we've been discussing has taken it into account, from othering to belonging, because this whole enterprise that we've been talking about, from good intentions to impact, that is also on this journey. The other thing we haven't talked about at all, I think since we've been in this dialogue, there are some Black Quakers who don't want to engage this way. They are very clear. Again, it's what we've said before: a third of them will do it, they're ready; a third we need to persuade, cajole, dialogue, talk.... [*He chuckles.*] I've met a third who are absolutely adamant... with quite a negative reaction. I say to people, if we leave groups, Whites-only groups, to do all the work as Whites, or we leave Blacks-only groups to do all the work as Blacks, at the end they are going to come up with their own version that may suit their own purposes, and it may be very good, but if we are talking interdependence, we've got to hammer out an interdependent way forward *together*.

Common Humanity

NN: There is no way able-bodied people just sit there and come up with policies for disabled people and just write a policy and set of practices and say, 'This is it....' The notion of common humanity, that's the one that gives me the courage to know... we have more in common than that which separates us. Until we recognise that, it's not about me against you, it's me and you *against the problem*. But people don't always recognise that.

I don't know how you see it, Jonathan, because I think the next step is.... I hope you don't mind packaging all the things and sending them to me like the first one you did. Whatever you send me, I'll be happy to see.

JD: I look at it now and think it's pretty good, raw material. I suppose we're moving towards thinking what to do with it now.

NN: Yeah.

JD: It needs further editing.

NN: Oh yes.

JD: We wouldn't want to send it out just as it is into the public domain, but quite a bit of it is good and interesting. It needs a good edit, to polish it and get it ready....

NN: Yes, yes....

We discussed the mechanics of editing and developing the transcripts of our conversations....

JD: You have one more question, number eight, and I have come up with ten in total.... I have looked at the later points, and they are less specific questions, they were more musings, and I was wondering if we were going to meet next week, if it might be a good idea to tidy up and combine all of my remaining points with your final question, if we could do it like that?

NN: Yes, sure.

8: The Books We Read, the Films We Watch, and the Music We Listen to: A Total Reorientation to Life 27 January, 2021

Nim's final discussion point:
- What new outlook on life as Quakers and as human beings are we, Jonathan and Nim, aiming at in moving from 'othering to belonging'?

Jonathan's final discussion points:
- Making commitment and allyship a daily reality – what are the challenges, the arguments against; but also, the benefits and the means of doing this?
- The power of listening and being listened to. We can create safe spaces for people to engage in active listening, free of fear or at least as free of fear as it is possible to be. I believe that this will be a powerful means to constructive action. Stories are vital. If there are different ways that people's stories can be heard and responded to, this will be potentially hugely beneficial.
- Language both positively and negatively defines discussions and discourse and the very way that we are with each other. Culture wars are often waged through and over language. One example of the power of language is the ongoing Quaker discussion around the term 'overseer' for people delivering pastoral support and oversight. This issue of language also connects with Nim's White female friend who declared herself terrified of 'saying the wrong thing'. There needs to be some sort of accepted lingua franca, where it is understood that there will not be linguistic perfection, but there is an agreed platform, albeit a shifting one, that allows for engagement, where

there are spaces built in for people to flag up issues and re-negotiate aspects of linguistic/conceptual terms of engagement.

Taking Pride in Our Achievements

We had some initial small talk about Jonathan's MA degree completion.

NN: Truth-telling is truth-telling, and if it's done in a way that is ethical and doesn't demean the self or the other, it is the right thing to do. Anyway.... So this is our last day on phase one, isn't it? Of this journey....

We then discussed the details of how to proceed with the project in terms of milestones, the order to complete tasks, and so on.

NN: At the end of the book that we are proposing to create, there needs to be a 'How to do...' course. It's not so prescriptive that you can't adapt it to your own situation, but it is a guiding principle that takes you through.... There are eight ways that have been documented, from the moment you encounter a racial issue, it's where people begin by defending their position, which is understandable. It's called socialisation, it's where people have been raised to think this country is the best in the world, my culture is the best.... That denial. Our course will begin by looking to move you from denial, and it is natural, because you've never been presented with this way. Then there is where you defend, even if you recognise other cultures, accept multiculturalism, you still defend.... Then the material will move you through the stages up to acceptance, adaptation, integration, all those stages. They're well mapped out. We can work with that when it comes to it, because we're building on work that has already been done....

JD: Right, so I've collated our questions at the start of the document that will become the transcript. I've put your final question and then my final three, points. I've realised that they're more observations, but they all seem to chime together. Your question about outlook on life, I think gathers up within it my points about commitment, allyship, power of listening, the importance of language. I have a feeling that they dovetail together. Would you like to get the ball rolling this week, because I think I started last week?

Moving from Othering to Belonging

NN: Yes.... I think we have to endeavour to simultaneously learn and unlearn a new way of being. When I think of the story of Jesus sitting at a well with a Samaritan woman, and she's saying, 'You Jews worship here, this way, we Samaritans worship this way.' Jesus was saying, 'There's another way. You can worship God in the spirit and in truth.' For me it is an orientation towards *life* that says we train ourselves. I don't believe people when they say 'I don't see colour', but I do believe you can go through a continuum where colour doesn't matter, and when colour doesn't matter, or sexuality doesn't matter, or gender doesn't matter. It doesn't mean you don't see it; it means that it does not dictate to you as a frame of reference how you relate to this person.

That is where equity comes into it, because it means you're relating to this person in their particularity, equally. You are not denying their particularity. If I am constructing a new house for myself, I'm going to put a ramp, because I know I have friends who use wheelchairs who will visit me. It's not an after-thought, because it's come to me from a place where I know how to treat people equitably, equally. As a Quaker, and a Quaker in Britain, because that's where we are located at the moment, the one-third we keep talking about who are reluctant to engage, some of whom belong to the older generation. I sometimes call them 'Yes, – it's enough!' That generation... we honour them. We need more engagement, but we don't expend our energies trying to recruit them. But we have to guard ourselves against ageism, because that's another -ism to avoid. But being realistic is knowing that this person, which isn't every older person of course, with their orientation, their socialisation, their pronouncement, they are so caught up historically, they glorify the Empire, Thatcherism, and all those things, and there's no way I'm going to have an interaction on race, multiculturalism, diversity, inclusion – I've got to avoid that. It's accepting who we become will be seen not in what we say, but in what we *do*.

The Work of a Lifetime

NN: A lot of people acquire training, racism awareness, gender awareness, sexuality awareness, as an accumulation of information. It doesn't seem to change their way of being, and for me it is where I am very clear in my mind. Stand-alone, one-off training, the Friends House bookshop having just one or two books on race, it won't work. It's where a person's bookshelf tells the story of this person's journey. Their reading, the films they watch, the music they listen to – it's a whole dimension. That philosophy also needs to be brought into our worship. What things do we have, what books in our libraries, in our Meeting Houses? It's a total re-orientation towards life, based on an inclusive mentality that is not acquired overnight. It's acquired through a process of learning and un-learning. That can only happen with the statement that has been made so many times and some people discount it and yet it is very important. 'Nothing about us, without us being present.'

In the end the Whites will not cut out a way of working with Blacks without Blacks being there, and Blacks may not be there at the beginning, but will have to be there at some point. The Blacks cannot work with Whites without including Whites in the dialogue. These 'silos' that put people in different camps... I think there is a third way: I'm going to talk about you, White person. I want you there when I'm talking about you. I'm going to talk about you, Disabled person, I want you there when we're having that conversation. This needs to happen – and it isn't a token presence. No White person who hasn't dealt with their defensiveness, no Black person who hasn't dealt with their anger, or is dealing with their anger, can be part of that third way of dialogue. It doesn't mean you have to be fully-formed, but you'll have un-learned some things and learned some other things, on your own, in order to continue the engagement. Defensiveness will be manageable and managed. That's why the topic comes up in some people. Because they haven't managed their anger or defensiveness it flares up, or people are afraid to bring it up, for fear that other people will flare up. When you come to it the hard way, you've dealt with those issues up to a point, and now you are willing to develop further. So, you have moved on from being a tenderfoot. That's the way I see it at the moment.

JD: All of this seems to relate back through so much of what we've been talking about, as well as indicating a potential way forward. It's the work of a lifetime, isn't it?

NN: Oh, yes.

JD: Your questions and your response, your thoughts about it just then, include what I've been mentioning about making commitment and allyship a daily reality, there are challenges to that. There are people who will argue against it, but ultimately there are clear means of doing it, and there are clear benefits if people *do* do it.

Community Work – and Pushback against It

JD: This morning I had another online meeting. Myself and my community development colleague met with a working group from the NHS. We're working on a project to generate feedback from BAME mothers in terms of how they feel about their maternity treatment before, during and after giving birth. So BAME mothers who have given birth in this area in the last six months, or who are expecting to give birth in the next few months are the key people who we're trying to get in touch with. Some have already responded to the online survey that we've published.

Towards the end of the meeting, two of the people attending remarked that this survey has gone out via various platforms, and that this link was shared on a community platform. I haven't seen that particular platform, or the feedback, but apparently a lot of the feedback that was then posted was incredibly negative. Some of it was general remarks like, 'Oh no, *another* survey!' which might just be an ungracious reaction to the fact that there's another survey. But apparently other people were posting other critical comments such as 'Why are you wanting feedback specifically from non-White people?' Stuff like 'Everyone matters, not just BAME mothers'. We talked about it, about possible actions against it.

My first reaction might be to feel my heart sink, but actually I think we just have to accept that it's there, we have to address it, and if we can find the right way or the right methods of addressing it, you can turn the tide on it. I'm a great believer in the power of water on stone, and it connects with your image of the three thirds, the three categories of mentality, and there will be a very obstinate, intransigent mentality. There are people who may seem like stone to begin with, but over time we can find a way through, but it takes strategy and tactics as well, to think about how to pitch it. I don't want to use the phrase 'knowing your enemy', but some of these people may see themselves as enemies of us, of what we want to achieve, but many others don't consciously see themselves in that way, they may be acting in certain ways for different reasons. It comes down to knowing your audience, and knowing that there are many different people in that audience, some more sympathetic, and others less sympathetic, and it's knowing that, knowing why they have that position, understanding that, and then feeding that back in to how we present all this, how we go about this work, so that we can win some more hearts and minds.

Gaining Psychological Permission

NN: I think it's very relevant. Some years ago, I was given a little money by the World Bank's office in Nairobi to work with subsistence farmers. We were doing participatory rural appraisal as an exercise in development. I had some students from the university. I contacted the community in Nakuru, men and women, about thirty of them. Told them we have fourteen days to work things out. I tell you, for the first three days they said nothing. They just took us here, there and everywhere, doing everything except what we wanted to do. They said to us, 'You're university people, you're educated, why are you asking us these questions? We know nothing, we never had the same schooling as you, what are you going to do with the information?' On the third day, I remember asking them, 'How many of you are parents?' Most of them. 'Do you have children? How old?' Some teenagers, older. I said, 'How many of your children have been in jail?' One or two. 'How many are going to university?' One or two. 'How many in secondary?' Most of them. I said, 'Do you know any Cabinet ministers whose children are in jail?' About twenty of them! I went on asking questions to show they were good parents who were able with very little to do a lot, and we went on from there to do good work.

But some points came very clearly out of that work that have helped me over the years when working with these communities. One thing to get into our minds, is how do we define a problem? A problem is a question in search of an answer. That for me when I looked at it that way, what I was encountering from these people, it wasn't about them blocking. I needed to perceive the situation as a question in search of an answer.

Another thing was legitimisation. When did we legitimise ourselves, and how have we gone about legitimising ourselves to this group? Because once we legitimise ourselves, we are accepted, they give us psychological permission to administer the survey, to tell them those things, to ask those questions. That is when the guard comes down, so when was the psychological permission given? When that is given, that confers credibility upon the speaker. What we say, they will listen to us, because they deem us credible. Part of legitimisation, is being with a member of the community, people who are known. That's why people use church members and community leaders and all that, who don't have to introduce themselves.

So, we have some key terms here: a problem is a question in search of an answer; legitimisation; psychological permission; credibility of the speaker. But it takes time. The quality of the work that we do and the quality of the work that comes from this is dependent on the depth of self-revelation, what people will let you see. They will let you see a little bit, depending on who you are. How do you legitimise yourself to a group of people, so that they can see you as a credible speaker? So that they will then give you the psychological permission to ask those questions. In this particular case, working in Nakuru is one of the things I learned. It's the same thing with the exercise we are doing. Some Meetings will be a challenge, some Meetings will want us to legitimise ourselves, and that's why I've been very clear in my mind about trying to place our work in the Quaker press, being at Woodbrooke, being in a publication that you can find in a Meeting House library. It might take a year, two years. There is a road along which people start dropping their guard and giving us the psychological permission to go to a Meeting and conduct a workshop or whatever.

The Importance of Listening
JD: I wonder if part of this also is about creating circumstances that facilitate different people, with different life experiences, being able to tell those life experiences, and also being able to hear the life experiences of others, in that open, non-judgemental, accepting atmosphere, and if there are ways that we might be able to facilitate that, and/or suggest techniques for people and groups

who want to do that. Because I think that's part of it as well, if people feel *listened to*, that's a lot of the struggle there. Of course, people have to act on that, having listened to and understood what people are telling them, they actually have to respond, they have to do something with it, they can't just let it disappear back out into the ether, but I think a lot of it is that act of listening and really paying attention to another person. I'm not sure if we could develop that as part of this course as well, maybe?

NN: Very much so. It is underpinned by the assumption that your story is legitimate. You have a legitimate story to tell. It might not be my story, but my story and your story are equally credible stories. Therefore that's why I listen to you, I give you the attention you deserve, and I'm listening to you because you are a credible person, with a credible story, and I care enough to listen. We are saying the purpose of listening to one another is to create a just society. That's what we are trying to do. Ultimately, we are creating a just society, and your story, my story, these are building blocks to do this. We're going to *listen*. Again, we've said before, contemplation without action, or just action without contemplation.... I have to think about why I am here with you and the Spirit, and the action will come out of that, it's not divorced from this. Everything we've been saying, we could do it as an action, even as an anti-racist action devoid of spirituality, devoid of contemplation, because it's about re-making the world, re-making society, re-making friends, in a totally different way. But for us there is also a spiritual element to it, and that makes it a spiritual activity as well. If it's divorced from that, it becomes just objective material that has no spiritual subjectivity, so you're right about the importance of listening.

Other Reading

JD: Just listening to what you're saying. It's just come in the post, so I still have to read it, but Audre Lorde's *The Master's Tools Will Never Dismantle the Master's House....*

NN: Yes, I have it in my reader here. It's a lovely essay.

JD: Something else that my instinct is telling me I must get on and read is Herbert Marcuse's *One-Dimensional Man*.

NN: Yes, I came across that a long time ago in sociology.... Something must have prompted you to want to read it?

JD: A while ago I read Herbert Marcuse's *Eros and Civilisation* and thought it was brilliant... that led me to get hold of this book. There's the notion of the Great Refusal in there, and also a model of social critique. As I understand him, Marcuse is very much arguing that in order to liberate society, we have to be critical readers of society and culture, and, also, we have to empower all those groups who are marginalised. Now I couldn't give a comprehensive list of all the groups who he views in that sense, but he certainly includes the young and students, but even if he doesn't explicitly say it, ethnic minority people are there, the workers are there, LGTBQ people are there, the disabled are there, and so on. It's because of that, really. My instinct is telling me that I need to go and equip myself with this model of social critique that he has in that book.

NN: Yes. Part of even Audre's work, and the other great writers of the past, it's how we read them with a post-modern mentality. Some of them were writing in the Modern era, some before then, and we need to consider to what extent a post-modern approach has re-shaped our thinking. It's post-modern, it's post-Christian, and it's multi-faith, non-faith... all these dimensions. Some things I read from that era help me. There's something I'm reading now, a recent work, it's by someone who doesn't believe in God, but it's an amazing book. He locates God in everything he says, he just doesn't use the 'God-word'! I can understand, this person has come to this awareness through a post-modern reading of the myth of a post-racial society with that framing narrative. There are people who are speaking, deeply – Rollo May[1] is one, a psychoanalyst, speaking deeply about the human condition.

It'll be interesting to hear your thesis, the narrative that you derive from Marcuse.

JD: Yes, I think that Marcuse links nicely with my final point about language and not taking things at face value, looking beneath the surface more, and the riches you get from that. Also, of course, becoming aware of those different patterns of control, tools of control and deception that are there.... He'll be worth reading, I think.

Worksheets

As explained previously, the following worksheets are intended to form the spine of a course of study, ideally for a group of seekers, up to a possible maximum of twelve. We suggest that sessions will run for between one hour and one and a half hours, beginning and ending with Quaker silence. The reading and research tasks should be assigned before the session, to pairs or small groups, for them to undertake some reading, research and thinking ahead of the session; they will then be able to feed back to the whole group and inform them of their new knowledge and insights, leading to further discussion and reflection. These worksheets are designed to offer a path for the group, from initially getting to know one another, familiarising ourselves with key concepts, historical events, and so forth, laying the groundwork for us to consider pathways to real and meaningful change, and our own personal roles in that process of change.

We will be very grateful if groups who use these worksheets can let us know via John Hunt Publishing how effective these worksheets are, and what changes if any they consider would be helpful.

NN and JD

Worksheet 1: Telling Your Story About Race
(Who are we engaging with?)

Considering how you understand your own racial background, when did you first become aware of 'race'? What does it mean to be a member of your particular racial/ethnic group(s) in the UK today?

Think back to a time in your life when you first noticed that people were different from you – that their skin was a different colour, or their hair looked different, etc. What do you remember about that time?

1. What is your earliest memory of having your first conversation around race? With whom? What context? Did something precede the conversation?
2. What did the significant adults do or say that helped you to understand and appreciate these differences?
3. What did the adults do that got in the way of your understanding and appreciating these differences?

- As we embark on this course of study and discussion together, where would you place yourself on the novice-activist scale?

Novice				Activist
1	2	3	4	5

Considering your reflection, what is the one new thing you have learned? What is the one action you're going to take?

Worksheet 2: Terminology, Language and Concepts
(What are we engaging with?)

Definitions matter, and communicating across cultures can be confusing and uncertain. Before committing to working towards creating change as anti-racist practitioners, we need to be clear what we mean by certain terms. Clarifying our language and terminology can help in opening up wider discussions about race and the importance of confronting discrimination.

What do the following words mean to you? How have they affected the way you think and feel about race and racism?

What has been your personal experience?

- Ally
- Anti-Racism
- Discrimination
- Implicit Bias
- Intersectionality
- Microaggression
- Prejudice
- Racism
- Racist Policies
- White Fragility
- White Privilege
- White Supremacy

Considering your reflection, what is the one new thing you have learned? What is the one action you're going to take?

Worksheet 3: Economics

1. How many of your work colleagues are/were Black?
2. What kinds of work do/did they have?
3. What are your perceptions of non-White people's experiences in the workplace?
4. How is the current situation affecting everyone, both Black and White?
5. If the situation was changed to become more inclusive, what would that new situation look and feel like?
6. How would it benefit everyone?
7. How could we support more genuinely inclusive cultures in our workplaces?

Considering your reflection, what is the one new thing you have learned? What is the one action you're going to take?

Worksheet 4: Social and Political Realities

Introductory Questions:

1. How many Black people do you know in your social situations? How do you happen to know them?
2. What do you *imagine* their social experiences are like? What do you *know* of their social experiences?
3. How would you react if you felt the potential for rejection and mistreatment regularly or constantly?

Research Tasks:

1. Compare White and Black experiences in the healthcare system, e.g., maternity care, Covid experience, death rates, etc.
2. Compare White and Black experiences of unjustified stop and search, arrest rates, deaths at the hands of police officers, deaths in custody.
3. Compare representation in: your local council; Parliament; Government; Cabinet. Consider numbers of representatives; how are White and Black experiences handled/responded to; how is official rhetoric applied to White and Black activities/experiences? Are there any areas of Black experience upon which the official record is silent?

Follow-up Questions:
1. How do we feel about what we have discovered?
2. Does anything need to change? If so, what?
3. What can I/we do to effect that change?

Considering your reflection, what is the one new thing you have learned? What is the one action you're going to take?

Worksheet 5: Case Studies: Dickerson and Dunbar

Mahala Ashley Dickerson and Barrington Dunbar offer two useful stories of Black people of faith who found their way to Quakers, and offered radical critiques of Quakerism. Dickerson in time moved on to other spiritual homes, whilst retaining friendships with Quakers and attending Meeting for Worship from time to time. Dunbar remained within the Society, whilst offering trenchant criticism of Quaker conduct and attitudes.

Below are brief biographies of these Quakers. Please read and discuss, with a focus on producing in response to their experiences:

- 1 comment;
- 1 question;
- 1 action.

Case Study 1: Mahala Ashley Dickerson
(1912–2007)

Mahala Ashley Dickerson, a pioneer in the fields of Law, racial justice and gender equality, was born in Alabama. She attended a private girls' school in Montgomery, and there made a life-long friendship with Rosa Parks. She graduated *cum laude* from two 'Black Ivy' universities: Fisk (in Sociology) and Howard (in

Law; she was one of only four women to graduate in the class of 1948) and achieved a series of notable career distinctions:

- The first African-American woman to be admitted to the Alabama Bar;
- The second African-American woman to be admitted to the Indiana Bar;
- The first African-American to be admitted to the Alaskan Bar;
- The first African-American to serve as President of the National Association of Women Lawyers.

Dickerson was no stranger to the prejudice and vagaries of subjective responses from different White people: on moving to Alaska with her triplet sons in 1958, she had her legitimate homestead claim refused by a clerk in Anchorage. Having studied the regulations closely overnight, she returned the next day ready to argue for her rights, only for a different clerk to file her claim without demur.

Raised as a Baptist, Dickerson became a pacifist and a Quaker after World War Two, whilst living in Indiana. In her memoirs she recalls a 1986 visit back to Indiana: 'I was able to renew contact with the Quakers, from whom I had received so much inspiration.'[1]

However, her memories are both positive and negative. She remembers that her formative Quaker experiences were in both programmed and unprogrammed contexts in Indiana, remarking that it was in 'the periods of silence' that one 'could get deep into your contemplation' which was 'what I had always thought of as Quaker.'[2]

On the other hand, she also includes some stinging memories of prejudice from within the Quaker community. The local Quaker minister in Indiana invited her and her family to join the 'Quaker church':

A minority of members objected to a black family joining their church. It seems the fact that they had built a beautiful new church in a high-priced neighbourhood was a major factor, as membership for black persons might cause a depreciation in property values.[3]

This caused Dickerson to wish to withdraw her application, but she was dissuaded from doing so by friends who 'wanted to see how everything would turn out'.[4] Dickerson's connections with Quakers held strong; she had spent a summer at Pendle Hill in 1950, and played a leading role in establishing Alaskan Friends Conference.[5] Johnny Gibbons, her law partner in Anchorage, has said, 'the principles that are held by Friends helped her become who she ultimately became, and it was a testament that the two were destined to be intertwined.'[6]

Throughout her life Dickerson had a varied spiritual life amongst different religious practices, stating, 'I have always had a deep abiding faith in God and cannot remember how it first came to me.... The contact with various religions through the years has probably left me a Quaptimethocat, Quaker, Baptist, Methodist, Catholic.' She also fondly recalls 'very pleasant contacts with the Baha'i's'.[7]

Dickerson moved on from Quakerism despite having initially felt that she had found her spiritual home, after overhearing a racist conversation about her by two weighty White Alaskan Friends:

My Quaker paradise was destined for trouble. In the same year that the American Bar Association was giving [me] one of its Margaret Brent Awards [Dickerson received this distinction in 1995; it is an honour that was also presented to Supreme Court Justices Ruth Bader Ginsburg in 1983 and Sandra Day O'Connor in 2000], I was destined to overhear racist remarks concerning me being made by Robert Sullivan and James Schiable, ranking Quakers, in my own home where they had been welcome to swim in my indoor heated pool. After that, Quakers were no longer welcome in my home but restricted to the meeting house area. I never felt quite the same, as the lack of sensitivity was obvious to me by this racist interchange, though it did not matter to the other members. Obviously, I am destined to worship alone and I feel that God understands.[8]

An observer could understand Dickerson's experiences to have made her feel rather lonely in her spiritual life, although she drew on them as a source of positive power. In a newspaper interview she remarked that, 'In my life, I didn't have but two things to do. Those were to stay black and to die. I'm just not afraid to fight somebody big.... Whenever there's somebody being mistreated, if they want me, I'll help them.'[9]

Awards and Distinctions:

- Doctor of Laws degree, University of Alaska, 1994;[10]
- Margaret Brent Award, American Bar Association, 1995;[11]
- Honor Kempton Award, Baha'i Assembly of Alaska;[12]
- Alabama State Bar's Maud McLure Kelly Award for outstanding female attorney, 2006;[13]
- The NAWL instituted the M. Ashley Dickerson Diversity Award in 2007 in her honour;[14]
- Dickerson's papers are held at the David M. Rubinstein Rare Book and Manuscript Library, Duke University, Durham, North Carolina, USA.[15]

Sources:

Weaver, Jr., H.D., Kriese, P. and Angell, S.W. (Eds.), (2011) *Black Fire: African American Quakers on Spirituality and Human Rights*, Philadelphia (PA): QuakerPress of Friends General Conference.

'Who was Mahala Ashley Dickerson?'; https://quakerspeak. com/video/who-was-mahala-ashley-dickerson/n.d.

Profile of Mahala Ashley Dickerson, *Anchorage Daily News*, n.d.

David Harmon (2011) 'Mahala Ashley Dickerson', *Encyclopedia of Alabama*, Alabama Humanities Foundation, accessed at http:// www.encyclopediaofalabama.org/article/h-1443.

Goldberg, S.B. (2005) 'Honoring the Unsung Heroes: Margaret Brent Awards Celebrate 15th Anniversary', American Bar Association, accessed at https://www.americanbar.org/ content/dam/aba/publishing/perspectives_magazine/women_ perspectives_HonoringUnsungHeroesSummer2005.pdf/.

'Mahala Ashley Dickerson'; Wikipedia; https://en.wikipedia. org/wiki/Mahala_Ashley_Dickerson#cite_note-11

Make notes here:

Case Study 2: Barrington Dunbar
(1901–1978)

Born into a poor family in British Guyana, Dunbar knew early that he was bright and had great potential. He received his primary schooling in Guyana and, owing to family necessity, left early to work as a tailor's apprentice. Craving self-development, he left for America at sixteen, following his older brother Rudolph, a professional musician, to Harlem. Once there, completing high school, he then availed himself of the no tuition-fee education that was then offered by New York City College, working at various jobs to fund himself.[14] He then went on to complete a Master's degree in Sociology at Columbia University before embarking on doctoral studies at the same institution, with a project titled 'The Difference in Behaviour Patterns of West Indian and Southern Negroes in Harlem'. However, noting the paucity of academic opportunities open to Black scholars, he withdrew from his Ph.D. to become the resident manager of a co-operative community in Greenwich Village.

Dunbar continued working in social and community projects, both in America and internationally. He managed work programmes in various locations around America and a guidance clinic for the New York Urban League, directed a displaced persons camp in Germany for the UN Relief and

Reconstruction Agency, organised refugee recreation in France and administered a yaws eradication programme in Haiti. Having become familiar with Quakers through his relief work in Europe, he joined the Society whilst living in Chicago in the period 1953–62, attending 57th Street Meeting. He later moved to New York City and attended 15th Street Meeting there. He was actively committed to both Quakerism and Black Liberation, and often challenged fellow Quakers over their levels of social engagement. The Black Power movement was, in his eyes, a legitimate reflection of 'a need to express rage as a step toward self-esteem'.[17] He bravely held a mirror up to Quakers, highlighting how their culture generally is successful in supporting and nourishing (mainly White, middle class) individuals, whilst often not fully grasping the harsh realities of life experienced by the (frequently Black) poor and excluded.

In a 1964 talk to the American Friends Service Committee, Dunbar offered nuanced praise to the AFSC's numerous support programmes with the caveat that Quakers had been able to articulate their views whilst not necessarily engaging in confrontation at national and international levels.[18]

Dunbar presents the stark binary choice that faces anyone of conscience, which is whether they will make common cause with the marginalised in challenging injustice, or else conspiring with their comfortable fellows in suppressing dissent.[19] He makes it plain that passive anti-racism is no anti-racism at all: either the individual engages directly in addressing patterns of injustice, or they remain inactive and disengaged and thus accepting of and complicit in those patterns of injustice. A point that is made increasingly frequently as a result of Black Lives Matter is that much White privilege – and the injustices that support it – remains comfortably invisible to the average White person. Dunbar sees and articulates this early on, implicitly facing his White audiences with a challenging question: if it is always true to say that unjust conditions are 'just the way they are', ask yourself, if you were someone who routinely found themselves belittled, exploited and erased yet knew yourself to be 'unique, precious, a child of God',[20] would you still be happy to accept the prevailing view that those oppressive conditions were 'just the way things are'?

Dunbar goes on to 'name the game' that is being played by many Quakers when it comes to potential conflict:

> Involvement in conflict and tension is so distasteful to some Friends that they may decide to remain neutral behind closed doors... [yet] each one of us, wherever we are, whatever our calling may be, as landlord, employer, teacher, neighbour, or citizen, must share the responsibility for removing the obstacles which stand in the way of so many of our fellow Americans from achieving the abundant life.[21]

In 1968 Dunbar published his first article in *Friends Journal*: 'Black Power's Challenge to Quaker Power', where he developed further his incisive analysis of White middle-class Quaker complicity in the *status quo*. Identifying and celebrating the holistic integration between the spiritual power of Quaker worship and the genuine commitment of practical action in the world, Dunbar goes on to bluntly state that much of that righteous fire has cooled:

> This close connection between work and worship – between the gathered community of the Meeting and the wider community – seems to be a missing ingredient in the practice of the Quaker Meeting today, which often tends to serve the purpose of a social club where people meet to pursue their common interests in isolation from the rest of the community.... Because our hearts are not stirred or our minds made sensitive to the injustices of the communities

in which we live, we accommodate ourselves to a whole system of personal and group relations... a system that has served to reinforce the assumption of White superiority. This way of life denies that there is that of God in every man, the vital message of Quakerism that provides the basis for the 'blessed community' in which everyone can achieve freedom from want and fear and can realize his full potential as a human being.[22]

When asked by an interviewer from *Friends Journal* if he found it difficult that many Quakers didn't grasp his intellectual support for the 'necessity of black rage', he replied, 'No, I don't mind.... Opposition means we are facing situations and each other. That's the way we progress. If everyone agreed, there would be no change in either of us.... We have to keep confronting situations and each other.'[23]

To anyone who might be tempted to confuse confrontation with aggression, he concluded that interview with this following remark about his spiritual modus operandi: 'If you love people, you can accomplish almost anything.'[24] Barrington Dunbar clearly accomplished much in his life. One online biography of him remarks, 'He was remembered affectionately for many years as an uncomfortable but vital "thorn in the side".'[25]

Distinctions:

- Attended Fourth World Conference of Friends at Greensboro, North Carolina (1967);
- New York Yearly Meeting renamed its Black Development Fund as The Barrington Dunbar Fund for Black Development.[24]

Sources:

'Barrington Dunbar' in *Quaker History Through Biographies*, https://www.fgcquaker.org/cloud/new-brunswick-friends-meeting-nyym/resources/quaker-history-through-biographies#BarringtonDunbar

'Quaker Portrait: Barrington Dunbar', Friends Journal, Friends Publishing Company, Philadelphia, PA, 1 May, 1970

Weaver, Jr., H.D., Kriese, P. and Angell, S.W. (Eds.), *Black Fire: African American Quakers on Spirituality and Human Rights*, QuakerPress of Friends General Conference, Philadelphia (PA), 2011

Make notes here:

Now, having reflected upon the experiences of two noted Black Quakers, we can consider the words of an inter-ethnic Quaker working group on their experiences....

Epistle from Black, White, Asian and Mixed-heritage Friends, 1991[27]

We recognise and celebrate what we as Black, Asian and mixed-heritage Friends [in Britain] bring to the Society and with pride we affirm our rich positive contributions. However, we find spoken and unspoken assumptions that because we are Black people we are economically needy, socially deprived, culturally disinherited and spiritually in need of Quaker instruction. We experience isolation both physical and spiritual within our meetings. It is not just a matter of numbers but without the active commitment to promote diversity within the Society of Friends it will continue to be difficult to foster a true experience of a spiritual community.

As Black and White Friends we recognise the importance of our children's needs to know and value themselves and the world around them with the love and support of a settled and secure family environment. We must all strive to ensure that race is not a barrier to our children's success. We need to look honestly and openly at the structure of our meetings and seek to broaden our experience of other enriching forms of worship. Quakerism enables us to face both the glory and seemingly unfaceable in ourselves. Let us do so now – together.

Questions to consider:
1. What might attract BAME worshippers to Friends?
2. What might force them away?

3. What can I do personally, and we do collectively, to welcome BAME people more fully (as well as other Members and Attenders)?
4. What can I and we do to make them feel more comfortable about staying?
5. What can we learn from our new arrivals?
6. What can we offer our new arrivals?

Finally, having discussed these different experiences and perspectives, are we ready to put together an action plan for how we might make our Meetings more open and welcoming places? Make some notes on a separate sheet....

Considering your reflection, what is the one new thing you have learned? What is the one action you're going to take?

Worksheet 6: Quaker 'Church' and Racism

Racism is a complex and enduring social problem that exists in many forms at institutional, interpersonal and individual levels and has done so for centuries. Regrettably, very little has changed and the sharp contrast between the churches' lofty ideals of 'the value of each person as a child of God' and the seemingly permanent second-class status of Black people in all walks of life.

We can work towards the elimination of the interconnected ways in which marginalization takes place and achieve greater unity across society by mobilising our churches in addressing race and racism in society.

In committing to transform our lives, our churches, and our society, we should acknowledge that we each have a different starting point.

- The Quaker concern for social inclusion arises from the belief that there is 'that of God' in everyone. However, about four in five of Black people are doubtful that the UK will ever achieve racial equality.

1. What do you think your church can do to confound the doubters of achieving equality?
2. What contribution can you yourself make?

Considering your reflection, what is the one new thing you have learned? What is the one action you're going to take?

Worksheet 7: Theology

Here are some key theological figures/key concepts which might be applicable to an emergent theology, for different people to familiarise themselves with, and come to the meeting ready to introduce to the group:

- Liberation Theology (Gustavo Gutierrez)
- The Great Refusal (Herbert Marcuse)
- Conscientization (Paulo Freire)
- *Realidad* and *praxis* (Marcella Althaus-Reid)
- Dialogism (Mikhail Bakhtin)

1. In what ways is the Divine trying to break through?
2. What do I need to refuse or relinquish in order for the excluded to have their portion? How can we consider our own context – our comforts and challenges, our observations of the experiences of others?
3. How might our consideration of the situation – and how it affects different people differently – raise us to consciousness?
4. What might a new, raised, consciousness look and feel like?
5. What might we feel inspired to do as a result?
6. Bakhtin argues that the one and the other need each other: 'I go out to the Other in order to come back with a Self.' We are defined through dialogue, so how are we going to seek that dialogue – and with whom? How might it change us?
7. Are we called to practise a 'Theology of Solidarity'? If so, what might this lead us to do? How might we change as a result of it?

Considering your reflection, what is the one new thing you have learned? What is the one action you're going to take?

Worksheet 8: Poetry and Creative Writing
Helen Morgan Brooks
(1904–1989)

Helen Morgan Brooks 'wrote with emotion and out of her own experience'.[1]

Her biography epitomizes an integrated life in the fullest sense, including both 'beauty and harshness, the glory and the horror'[2] as well as the practical and creative. The eldest of six children of a barber and a home-maker, she was born in Reading, Pennsylvania. As a result of financial difficulties faced by the family following their relocation to Philadelphia, Brooks was placed in care for six years. Despite these challenging circumstances, she secured a Higher Education, graduating with a B.A. in Home Economics from St Augustine College, North Carolina, at the age of twenty, later studying Education at Temple University.

She initially worked as a dietician and latterly as a Home Economics teacher in the Philadelphia school system. Alongside her well respected and prize-winning poetry, she also wrote *One Person, One Meal, One Burner*, a practical guide about how people on a restricted budget of $5 a week could feed themselves, evidencing an astuteness in offering down-to-earth advice for dealing with difficult circumstances. In the 1940s she received a fellowship to Pendle Hill, where she taught, wrote and cooked. She formally joined the Religious Society of Friends in 1956, at the age of 52.

Brooks' poetry demonstrates a powerful integration of darkness and light, of the concrete and the conceptual. She won various prizes for her poetry, for example, the Poundstone, Delaware Poetry Society and Wilmington Poetry Society Awards, and was anthologized in *New Negro Poets USA* (1964) edited by Langston Hughes and *The Poetry of the Negro, 1749–1970*, edited by Hughes and Arna Wendell Bontemps. She was also the editor of the poetry magazine *Approach*.

Her work addresses a broad range of concerns, from the spiritual to the practical, from the harshly realistic to the noumenal, exemplifying how one person can seek to integrate different urges and qualities within their own art. Shortly before her death from cancer at the age of 85, she remarked to her sister, 'I simply want to sit out on the beach and watch the wonder of the rain, smell its fragrance and marvel at the miracle of God's works.'[3]

Academic Diane Reynolds argues that Brooks' poetry offers a powerful vision that speaks to modern-day Quaker concerns:

'Helen Morgan Brooks... speaks from the perspective of the marginalized and also offers a way forward to an articulation of a Quaker experience that critiques and spills beyond the boundaries of White middle-class cultural norms.'[4]

'Depicting faith as the cry of a suffering humanity rather than a quaint, antiquarian artifact.'[5]

'Rather than try to impose a normalizing morality on us, Brooks invites us into a world of ugliness and beauty, cruelty and grace, pain and love, not a false, enamel world where pain has been removed, but a real world in which God moves among the suffering.'[6]

Now let's consider some of Brooks' poetry...

As we read and discuss it, you can think about poetic technique, the cumulative power of her poetry, and how it speaks directly to you in your own context. Try to identify:

- 1 comment
- 1 question
- 1 action

in response to her work, either to the poem extracts presented here, or one set of responses to the poems as a whole.

For a concise evocation of Quaker worship that recalls something of the sense of haiku, read 'Meeting for Worship'.[7] This poem concludes with the implied worshipper being enfolded by the Divine within the worshipping silence that was 'expecting us/ when we entered'.

'Slum House'[8] offers a powerful snapshot of the corrosive effects of poverty and marginalisation, where filth and squalor abound, and 'liquor fumes stalk/the stairs like demented ghosts...'

'Black Child'[9] meditates on the complex nature of the experience of being Black in a White majority society that ignores the variety of skin tones that include 'honey'/'sunsets lowering,'/'[and] Autumn leaves,...'

1. How do these poems make you feel? Do you have any sense of a 'spilling over'?
2. What elements of 'ugliness and beauty, cruelty and grace' can you find in them?
3. How do these poems speak to you of the marginalized?
4. In what ways does HMB express faith as a 'cry of suffering humanity'? How might we become more aware of the experience of 'suffering humanity' around us?

5. Do any of these poems offer spiritual insight or transformation to you?

Writing activity:[10]

- Try listening to three different pieces of music/other sound recordings. For instance, you could use a protest song, like 'We Shall Overcome' or 'Bread and Roses', some other, less political, but powerfully emotive music, and a recording of an activity or event, or real life (e.g., people having a conversation, a street protest, a news broadcast, etc.).

- As you listen to each of the three recordings, jot down your responses to the following prompts. Try not to reflect too much upon them at this point; just get them down!

1. First recording:
   a. What do you see when you're listening? Write it down.
   b. How does it make you feel? Note that down.
   c. Now write a sentence for this image and emotion. It could be poetry, prose, drama...

2. Second recording:
   a. Write down a different feeling.
   b. Scribble down another first line.
   c. Now, what is the visual image that is suggested to you by this recording? Note that as well.

3. Third recording – perhaps close your eyes; certainly, listen closely. Then:

a. Write down a new first line.

b. How are you feeling this time? Make a note.

c. Jot down the visual image that is being suggested to you.

4. Now, share the materials in your group, and spend some time working with what you have written. Is there material here for your own poem, story, play? Or some other kind of action? How might it relate to our case study of Helen Morgan Brooks?

Considering your reflection, what is the one new thing you have learned? What is the one action you're going to take?

Worksheet 9: A Community of Practitioners

The community of anti-racist practitioners share a passion for social justice; it is made up of Black and White people who meet regularly to explore the effect and practices of racism over a sustained period of time in order to learn how to do it better. They reject and oppose the saying, *equality is always proclaimed but never realised.*

These people have experienced the power of solidarity and allyship and are ready to face the enormity of the challenges that face our planet and our marginalised communities. They come together to create a space that is authentic to everyone's experiences by acknowledging that racism impacts our lives differently depending on our social standing and which group we belong to.

It is acknowledged among the practitioners that the responsibility of challenging racism should not fall to Black members only, but their personal perspective and particular understanding and experience of racism are considered closely.

- What resources can we draw from the community to form an anti-racist community of practitioners working towards creating an equal and just society?
- What would 'The Community of Practitioners' toolkit contain as guidelines?

As we move towards the end of this particular stage of our journey as anti-racism practitioners where would you place yourself on the novice-activist scale, and why?

Novice				Activist
1	2	3	4	5

Considering your reflection, what is the one new thing you have learned? What is the one action you're going to take?

We often think about racism as individual acts of discrimination on the basis of race that happen between individuals or groups. However, Cultural Racism and Structural Racism (sometimes also referred to as institutional racism) powerfully shape racial disparities and outcomes. The concept of equity is synonymous with fairness and justice. However, equity is not just about one-to-one relationships, but also works in terms of structural and systemic racism that inform assumptions of White superiority in everyday thinking. For example, mono-cultural organizational culture of shared assumptions, values, and beliefs, which govern how people are treated in employment practices including in pay and conditions, promotions etc.

- Reflect on a time when you saw, experienced or were told about an account of 'interpersonal' racism. What elements of cultural or structural racism might have enabled that behaviour to occur?

We are now going to spend some time in worship-sharing.
Before the silence...
If anyone has brought a reading, from *Quaker Faith & Practice* or any other appropriate source, please feel free to share it.
After the silence...
Is there anything in your mind or on your heart that you believe has been laid there by the Spirit, that you wish to share?

Considering your reflection, what is the one new thing you have learned? What is the one action you're going to take?

Final Feedback...

Rating your experience on the course:

- What has gone well? Why?

- What has not gone so well? Why?

- What would you like to see being done differently next time?

Change is incremental, and racism will exist long after I die. But if you're committed to anti-racism, you're in it for the long haul. It will be difficult. Getting to the end point will require you to be uncomfortable.

Reni Eddo-Lodge, *Why I'm No Longer Talking to White People about Race*

Nim Njuguna is a retired Baptist minister and former Quaker prison chaplain and restorative justice trainer. He writes on inclusion, spirituality and diversity in a wide range of Quaker and other periodicals. His 1995 PhD thesis was on 'Racism, Black Marginality, the Labour Party and Church of England in the 1980s'. He also offers spiritual accompaniment and supervision informed by liberation theologies and person-centred therapeutic perspectives. He has taught at the London Centre for Spirituality, been an associate chaplain at Anglia Ruskin University, and is a lifetime member of 'Spiritual Directors Europe'. He completed Woodbrooke's Equipping for Ministry Course and was an Eva Koch scholar in 2018. He has held various Quaker roles, including committee member of Quaker World Relations and representative to Meeting for Sufferings. He has been involved with a variety of local and area Quaker meetings on developing their inclusion practices. A long-time resident of North London and member of Harrow Local Meeting, Nim has recently returned to live in Kenya with his wife Liz. They currently attend Johannesburg Meeting online.

Jonathan Doering has been a Quaker for nearly twenty years, and has worked mainly in sixth form and further education, and community development with a special focus on racial equality and integration. He has served in a variety of Quaker capacities, including Elder, representative to Meeting for Sufferings, and Local Meeting Assistant and Co-Clerk. He holds Master's degrees in Creative Writing and Quaker Studies, and his MA thesis on Quaker poetry was recently published in *Quaker Studies* journal. Jonathan has published fiction, poetry and journalism in various newspapers and magazines, including: *The Friend, Quaker Voices, Christians Aware, Faith Initiative, Concrete, Bucket of Tongues, Cascando, Icarus, LitSpeak, Poetry Manchester, Backdrop, Contemporary Review, AltHist, Brittle Star, Gold Dust* (winning a

Best Prose Award), *The Guardian*, and *The Green Parent*. His SF e-novella, *Eurworms*, is available online. Jonathan lives with his family in Nottingham and is a member of Nottingham Local Meeting.

From Nim and Jonathan: Thank you for purchasing *Enlarging the Tent*. We sincerely hope that you have gained as much from reading it as we have in creating it. If you have a few moments, please feel free to add your review of *Enlarging the Tent* at your favourite online site for feedback. Also, if you would like to connect with other books that we have coming in the near future, please visit our Facebook pages, or at: jnshabash@gmail.com and monikajonathan1@gmail.com

Sincerely, Nim Nuguna and Jonathan Doering.

Endnotes

Introduction

[1] Fox, G. (1647) *Journal*, collected in *Quaker Faith and Practice*, Chapter 19, 'A gathered people', 19.03.

[2] See 'BAME deaths in police custody', https://www.inquest.org.uk/bame-deaths-in-police-custody, accessed 11 June, 2022. These statistics record fifty-nine deaths of People of Colour at the hands of British Police in the last decade.

[3] See Das, S. 'Met rebuked for strip searches two years before Child Q case in Hackney', 20 March, 2022, *The Observer Online*, https://www.theguardian.com/uk-news/2022/mar/20/met-rebuked-for-strip-searches-two-years-before-child-q-case-in-hackney, accessed 11 June 2022; also, Francis, A., 'Child Q: Met Police officers strip-search thousands of children and majority are from ethnic backgrounds', 25 March, 2022, archived at *I-news*, https://inews.co.uk/news/child-q-met-police-strip-search-children-majority-ethnic-backgrounds-1539008, accessed 11 June, 2022.

Dialogue 1

[1] At the time of going to press, the authors are aware that there is an ongoing discussion around this issue. For instance, see the *Friends Journal* article, FJ News Editors, 'William Penn's name removed from room in London's Friends House', May 5, 2021, accessed at: https://www.friendsjournal.org/william-penns-name-removed-from-room-in-londons-friends-house/

[2] See Nim's article on Allyship in *The Friends Quarterly*, Issue 1, 2020.

[3] For Enoch Powell's speech regarding the mistreatment of suspected Mau Mau fighters by British forces in Kenya, see Heffer, S., 301–305. In acknowledging that Powell made an admirable speech in 1959 condemning racist British behaviour, we in no way wish to suggest that this off-sets the damage and hurt caused by his later notorious 'rivers of blood' speech in 1968, which did so much to rhetorically burnish the image of racism within Britain.

[4] The Profumo Scandal in 1963 centred on the extra-marital relationship between then Defence Secretary John Profumo (1915–2006) and Christine Keeler (1942–2017), who also was in a relationship with a Russian Naval attaché. For further background, there is a wide range of sources, including: Davenport-Hines, R. (2013) *An English Affair: Sex, Class and Power in the Age of Profumo*. London: William Collins; also, Knightley, P., Kennedy, C. (1987) *An Affair of State: The Profumo Case and the Framing of Stephen Ward*, London: Jonathan Cape.

[5] Helen Suzman (1917–2009) was the only Progressive Party MP in the South African parliament for thirteen years. She frequently faced misogynistic and anti-Semitic abuse during her career as an MP fighting racism and oppression. Her personal motto was said to be: 'Go and see for yourself.' For further background, see, for example, 'Obituary: Helen Suzman', BBC News, 1 January 2009, accessed at: http://news.bbc.co.uk/1/hi/world/africa/1694056.stm

[6] Eamonn Casey (1927–2017) had been a progressive Bishop of Galway and Kilmacduagh before various allegations of sexual abuse and misconduct left his reputation in tatters. See, amongst other sources, Sheehy, C. 'Profile: The larger-than-life Bishop at the centre of a scandal that rocked Ireland', *Irish Independent*, 13 March, 2017.

Dialogue 2

[1] Pete Buttigieg (b. 1982) is an American Democrat politician and the first openly gay Cabinet minister, currently serving as President Joe Biden's Secretary of Transportation. Previous to this he made a name for himself as Mayor of South Bend, Indiana. For further information see, amongst other reports, O'Connell, O., 'Pete Buttigieg becomes first openly gay cabinet member after historic Senate vote', *The Independent*, February 2, 2021, archived at: https://www.independent.co.uk/news/world/americas/us-politics/pete-buttigieg-openly-gay-cabinet-member-senate-b1796535.html

Dialogue 3

[1] See Njuguna, N., 'Considering Equality and Truth: Nim Njuguna Explores Three Mindsets', *The Friend*, 20 May 2021.

Dialogue 4

[1] Njuguna, N., 'Spiritual Direction from the Closet to the Marketplace', *SPIDIR Newsletter*, Autumn 2020, Edition 98, pp. 8–10.

Dialogue 5

[1] ESOL stands for English for Speakers of Other Languages. Whereas EFL (English as a Foreign Language) is broadly aimed as a more self-consciously academic version of English for non-native speakers, ESOL is aimed more at immigrants, refugees and asylum seekers who need to learn English for everyday purposes, although of course in time they may well move on to seek higher-level academic qualifications.

[2] Gutierrez, G. *A Theology of Liberation*.

[3] This organisation, established by Quakers, does excellent work with young people in a variety of settings to help them to address

feelings of anger and aggression in a positive and constructive way. For more information see https://leapconfrontingconflict. org.uk/

[4] Matthew Fox is a former Dominican priest, theologian, writer and academic, who came into conflict with the Roman Catholic hierarchy over various aspects of his interpretations of traditional Catholic teachings, such as Original Sin. He came into direct conflict with the then Cardinal Joseph Ratzinger (later Pope Benedict XVI) when Ratzinger was head of the Vatican's Congregation of the Doctrine of the Faith. Ratzinger found fault with various tenets within Fox's teachings, including feminist attitudes, a refusal to condemn homosexuality, and a rejection of 'Original Sin' in preference for a concept of 'Original Blessing'. Since his resulting expulsion in 1993, Fox has become a priest in the American Episcopalian Church. His work now combines elements of traditional Christianity with ecology, goddess worship and various other non-mainstream practices and schools of thought. Amongst many plaudits that he has received is the remark by Dom Bede Griffith, Order of Saint Benedict that '[Fox's] creation spirituality is the spirituality of the future and his Theology of the Cosmic Christ is the theology of the future' (extract from 'Spirituality for a New Era: Dialog with Matthew Fox and Bede Griffiths', September 1992, recorded at Holy Names College, Oakland, California). Further information available from: Vallalongo, Fred and Sally, 'Matthew Fox confronts life outside the Catholic Church', 'New Age', *The Toledo Blade,* 28 March 1993; 'Fascism in the Church: Ex-Priest on "The Pope's War," Clergy Abuse and Quelling Liberation Theology'*Democracy Now!,* February 28, 2013; Watanabe, Teresa. 'Seeking the Feminine in God: Goddess worship accentuates female origins of the Almighty', *The Los Angeles Times,* November 3, 1998.

[5] For further information, for example, see: 'Amelia Lapeña-Bonifacio', *The World Encyclopaedia of Puppet Arts* online, archived at: https://wepa.unima.org/en/amelia-lapena-bonifacio/, accessed 8 June, 2022; Casper, L., (1983). 'The Opposing Thumb: Recent Philippine Literature in English', *Pacific Affairs*, 56 (2): 301–309.

[6] For instance see: Grady, D., 'H. Jack Geiger, Doctor Who Fought Social Ills, Dies at 95', *The New York Times*, December 28, 2020; 'In memoriam: H. Jack Geiger, Professor Emeritus CUNY School of Medicine and community health pioneer', ccny.cuny.edu, The City College of New York, archived at https://www.ccny.cuny.edu/news/memoriam-h-jack-geiger-professor-emeritus-cuny-school-medicine-and-community-health-pioneer, accessed 8 June, 2022.

[7] 'Theopraxis (Theos: God and praxis: practice) affirms the full presence, the experience, and a personal relationship with God. The emphasis is on the way a living relationship with God transforms life in the here and now.' From 'Theology or Theopraxis', available at http://chatswithgod.com/chat/2015-01-08-theology-or-theopraxis-6042556/index.html, accessed 02/04/2022.

Dialogue 7

[1] A prominent White American Quaker who has become an ally of Quakers of colour, discussed at the start of Dialogue 6, page 56.

[2] See Murgatroyd, L., 'Perhaps textile art can be a form of prophecy?', *The Friend*, Volume 178, No. 3, 17 January 2020.

[3] For the material that we discuss here, please see the Worksheets of this book.

Dialogue 8

[1] Rollo Reece May (1909-1994). American existential psychologist also connected with humanistic psychology and existential philosophy. He was closely associated with both psychotherapist Viktor Frankl and theologian Paul Tillich. His celebrated 1969 book, *Love and Will,* ponders humanity's search for meaning in modern life, and the relationship between the forces of love and will.

Worksheet 5

[1] Dickerson, M.A., *Delayed Justice for Sale: An Autobiography,* 144–47.

[2] Dickerson, 189.

[3] Dickerson, 190.

[4] Dickerson, 190.

[5] See 'Who was Mahala Ashley Dickerson?'; https://quakerspeak. com/video/who-was-mahala-ashley-dickerson/; posted April 1, 2021.

[6] Quoted in 'Who was Mahala Ashley Dickerson?'; https:// quakerspeak.com/video/who-was-mahala-ashley-dickerson/; posted April 1, 2021.

[7] Dickerson, 191.

[8] Dickerson, 192.

[9] Profile of Mahala Ashley Dickerson, *Anchorage Daily News,* https://www.adn.com/alaska-life/2020/01/19/pioneer-alaska-lawyer-dickerson-dies-at-94/ , n.d.

[10] Harmon, D. (2011) 'Mahala Ashley Dickerson', *Encyclopedia of Alabama*, Alabama Humanities Foundation, accessed at http://www.encyclopediaofalabama.org/article/h-1443.

[11] Goldberg, S.B. (2005) 'Honoring the Unsung Heroes: Margaret Brent Awards Celebrate 15th Anniversary', American Bar Association, accessed at https://www.americanbar.org/content/dam/aba/publishing/perspectives_magazine/women_perspectives_HonoringUnsungHeroesSummer2005.pdf/.

[12] Referred to in Dickerson, 191.

[13] Harmon, D. (2011) 'Mahala Ashley Dickerson', *Encyclopedia of Alabama*, Alabama Humanities Foundation, accessed at http://www.encyclopediaofalabama.org/article/h-1443.

[14] "M. Ashley Dickerson Diversity Award Recipients", National Association of Women Lawyers website, accessed at https://www.nawl.org/p/cm/ld/fid=71

[15] Duke University Libraries, *Guide to the Mahala Ashley Dickerson Papers, 1958–2007 and undated*, Durham, North Carolina: Duke University.

[16] 'Barrington Dunbar' at *Quaker History Through Biographies*, https://www.fgcquaker.org/cloud/new-brunswick-friends-meeting-nyym/resources/quaker-history-through-biographies#BarringtonDunbar.

[17] 'Barrington Dunbar', ed. Paul Kriese, in Weaver, Jr., H.D., Kriese, P. and Angell, S.W. (Eds.), 125.

[18] See Dunbar, B., 'The Society of Friends and the Negro Revolution', collected in Weaver, Kriese, and Angell: 126.

19 See Dunbar, B., 'The Society of Friends and the Negro Revolution', collected in Weaver, Kriese, and Angell: 126.

20 The Yearly Meeting of the Religious Society of Friends (Quakers), *Quaker Faith and Practice*, 1.02.22.

21 Dunbar, B., 'The Society of Friends and the Negro Revolution', collected in Weaver, Kriese, and Angell: 126–7.

22 Dunbar, B. 'Black Power's Challenge to Quaker Power', *Friends Journal*, Friends Publishing Company, Philadelphia, PA, Vol. 14, No. 18, 15 September, 1968: 460.

23 'Quaker Portrait: Barrington Dunbar', *Friends Journal*, Friends Publishing Company, Philadelphia, PA, Vol. 16, No. 9, 1 May, 1970: 258.

24 'Quaker Portrait: Barrington Dunbar', *Friends Journal*, Friends Publishing Company, Philadelphia, PA, Vol. 16, No. 9, 1 May, 1970: 258.

25 'Barrington Dunbar' in *Quaker History through Biographies*, https://www.fgcquaker.org/cloud/new-brunswick-friends-meeting-nyym/resources/quaker-history-through-biographies#BarringtonDunbar

26 See 'Barrington Dunbar' in *Quaker History through Biographies*, https://www.fgcquaker.org/cloud/new-brunswick-friends-meeting-nyym/resources/quaker-history-through-biographies#BarringtonDunbar

27 An excerpt from *Worship without prejudice?: an information pack on race relations within the Religious Society of Friends*, 1992, included in *Quaker Faith and Practice*, 29:15.

Worksheet 8

[1] Weaver, Jr., H.D., Kriese, P. and Angell, S.W. (Eds.), 139; the bulk of biographical detail used in this section derives from their chapter on Brook, pp. 139–150. Certain details regarding poetry awards won have been taken from Sandman, G., *Quaker Artists*, 105.

[2] Reynolds, D., 'Quakers and Fiction: Towards Breaking out of the Backward Gaze', 80–9, in James W. Hood, (Ed.), 86.

[3] From 'Introductory Remembrance', Brooks, H.M., *I Choose Love*, 1990.

[4] Reynolds, 85–6.

[5] Reynolds, 86.

[6] Reynolds, 86.

[7] See 'Women's History Month and Helen Morgan Brooks', *The Black Quaker Project*, posted 4 March, 2021, available at: https://www.theblackquakerproject.org/post/women-s-history-month-helen-morgan-brooks , accessed 29 June, 2022.

[8] Collected in Weaver, Jr., H.D., Kriese, P. and Angell, S.W. (Eds.), 142–3.

[9] See 'Women's History Month and Helen Morgan Brooks', *The Black Quaker Project*, posted 4 March, 2021, available at: https://www.theblackquakerproject.org/post/women-s-history-month-helen-morgan-brooks , accessed 29 June, 2022.

[10] This activity slightly reworks a writing exercise from Ali Smith's excellent contribution to Julia Bell and Paul Magrs' extremely useful *Creative Writing Coursebook*, 2001.

Further Reading

There is a large and growing body of work on racism and responses to it. We offer here a taster list of books, some Quaker or other-religiously themed and others secular, which we have found useful thus far. Some deal with historical issues, others with current social ones; others offer philosophical and theological input, sometimes specifically within the frame of addressing racism, sometimes more broadly when considering oppression more generally. If readers have not tried these books and websites, we offer them as further possibilities. Please let us know if they have been useful and interesting – and please pass on your own reading recommendations!

Baldwin, J. (1990) *The Fire Next Time*, London: Penguin Classics – a great Afro-American writer sets down his thoughts on the race situation. Written in the 1960s, it is still a study of deep dignity and thought.

Cooper, T. (2021) *Queer and Indecent*, London: SCM Press – is an introduction to the notoriously complex theological work of Marcella Althaus-Reid, first woman professor of theology at Edinburgh University. Althaus-Reid was particularly concerned with how the Church could become more accepting of women and LGBTQ people, but her call for a truly inclusive praxis speaks across different people's experiences.

Dabiri, E. (2021) *What White People Can Do Next: From Allyship to Coalition*, London: Penguin Books – Dabiri offers a pithy and cogent primer on the history of racism, with some challenging and provocative suggestions for how we can move forward.

DiAngelo, R. (2018) *White Fragility*, London: Penguin – outlines how racism isn't just a practice limited to 'bad' people – an essential corrective to comfortable middle-class evasion tactics.

Eddo-Lodge, R. (2017) *Why I'm No Longer Talking to White People about Race*, London: Bloomsbury – offers useful differentiation of British African and Afro-Caribbean experience, and the understandable frustration of Black people in a White society tainted by racism.

Fanon, F. (2021 *Black Skin, White Masks*, London: Penguin Modern Classics – Born in the French colony of Martinique, Fanon served as a soldier in the Free French Forces in World War Two before training as a doctor and psychiatrist. Widely regarded as his magnum opus, this collection of essays explores the insidious tools of oppression brought to bear on Black people by White, imperialist systems.

Fanon, F. (2001) *The Wretched of the Earth*, London: Penguin Modern Classics – Fanon brought his medical and psychiatric training to bear on his understanding of racism as a disease afflicting everyone affected by it. Paulo Freire was partly dialoguing with this text when he wrote his classic *Pedagogy of the Oppressed*.

Freire, P. (1996) *Pedagogy of the Oppressed*, London: Penguin Books – Freire is primarily concerned with the socio-economically oppressed, but his message of *conscientization* – raising to consciousness – again speaks to all conditions and is a vital addition to any activist's tool kit.

Gutierrez, G. (2018) *A Theology of Liberation*, NY: Orbis Books – for those who want a theological underpinning for their activism, this is one of the foundational classics.

Holquist, M. (1990) *Dialogism: Bakhtin and his World*, London: Routledge. Bakhtin's work is famously brilliant and abstruse, covering a wide range of theory, from literary studies through linguistics to theology and philosophy. Holquist's primer offers a clear and concise summary of some of his main ideas. Bakhtin's foregrounding of the importance of dialogue and connection within experience is key.

hooks, b. (1994) *Teaching to Transgress*, Abingdon, Oxon.: Routledge. This book, written by hooks in dialogue with Freire's *Pedagogy*, brings a Black 'queer-pas-gay' woman's perspective to liberational praxis.

Khan, S. (2010) *Creative Community Organizing: A Guide for Rabble-Rousers, Activists and Quiet Lovers of Justice*, San Francisco, CA: Berret-Koehler Publishers, Inc. – a seasoned activist, musician, and founder of the progressive Grassroots Leadership organisation, Khan offers an accessible handbook for those who want to take action.

Liebmann, M. (2004) *Arts Approaches to Conflict*, London: Jessica Kingsley Publishers – offers a range of approaches to dealing with situations of conflict positively. Several of the contributors have Quaker backgrounds.

Lorde, A. (2007) *Sister Outsider*, London: Penguin Modern Classics – Lorde was a poet, teacher and activist, and these identities are woven through the articles and essays in this book. Every phrase is weighted with meaning and poetic craft.

Marcuse, H. (2002) *One-Dimensional Man*, Oxford: Routledge Classics – a Jewish refugee from Nazi Germany, Marcuse saw the future of dissent and revolution as lying amongst groups marginalised by mainstream society.

Jr. Weaver, H.D., P. Kriese, S.W. Angell, (Ed.s) (2011), *Black Fire: African American Quakers on Spirituality and Human Rights*, Philadelphia, PN: Quaker Press of Friends General Conference – this powerful anthology includes work by a series of key Afro-American Quakers, including Helen Morgan Brooks, Mahala Ashley Dickerson and Barrington Dunbar who feature in our worksheets – and also Benjamin Banneker, son of a freed slave and an astronomer, author Jean Toomer, key civil rights activist Bayard Rustin, and Bill Sutherland who worked alongside peaceful revolutionists in Southern Africa, amongst many others.

There is a huge amount of material on the internet, sometimes of variable quality and use. The interested researcher can find much of relevance and interest by searching the website of Britain Yearly Meeting at: https://www.quaker.org.uk/; just one of many one incisive pieces details the frustrations of being a member of the Black Global Majority in a White majority society: https://www.quaker.org.uk/blog/a-response-to-black-lives-matter-by-a-bgm-quaker

Other web-based sources of interest include:

TheBlackQuakerProject at https://www.theblackquaker project.org/ which offers a wide range of reading materials and recordings of talks and films for the enquirer to download, read and view.

The American Quaker publication *Friends Journal* also has a broad archive of pieces relating to racism, available at: https://www.friendsjournal.org/issue-category/2021/race-and-antiracism/. Kathleen Bell has published an insightful article on the flawed legacy of William Penn with *Friends Journal*, available here: https://www.friendsjournal.org/flawed-quaker-heroes/

Bibliography

'Amelia Lapeña-Bonifacio', *The World Encyclopaedia of Puppet Arts* online, archived at: https://wepa.unima.org/en/amelia-lapena-bonifacio/, accessed 8 June, 2022.

'BAME deaths in police custody', https://www.inquest.org.uk/bame-deaths-in-police-custody, accessed 11 June, 2022.

'Barrington Dunbar' at *Quaker History Through Biographies*, https://www.fgcquaker.org/cloud/new-brunswick-friends-meeting-nyym/resources/quaker-history-through-biographies#BarringtonDunbar, 2017, accessed 11 June, 2022.

BBC News, 'Obituary: Helen Suzman', 1 January 2009, http://news.bbc.co.uk/1/hi/world/africa/1694056.stm accessed ln 11 June 2022.

Bell, J. and Magrs, P. (Eds.) *The Creative Writing Coursebook*, London: Macmillan, 2001.

Black Quaker project, The, 'Women's History Month and Helen Morgan Brooks', posted 4 March, 2021, available at: https://www.theblackquakerproject.org/post/women-s-history-month-helen-morgan-brooks, accessed 29 June, 2022.

Britain Yearly Meeting, *Quaker Faith & Practice*. London: The Religious Society of Friends (Quakers) in Britain, 1999 [1995].

Brooks, H.M., *I Choose Love*, Philadelphia, PA: Pendle Hill Publications, 1990.

Casper, L., (1983). 'The Opposing Thumb: Recent Philippine Literature in English', *Pacific Affairs*, 56 (2).

Das, S. 'Met rebuked for strip searches two years before Child Q case in Hackney', 20 March, 2022, *The Observer Online*, https://www.theguardian.com/uk-news/2022/mar/20/met-rebuked-for-strip-searches-two-years-before-child-q-case-in-hackney, accessed 11 June 2022.

Davenport-Hines, R. *An English Affair: Sex, Class and Power in the Age of Profumo*. London: William Collins, 2013.

Dickerson, M.A., *Delayed Justice for Sale*, Anchorage, Alaska: Al-Acres Inc.: 1998.

Profile of Mahala Ashley Dickerson, *Anchorage Daily News*, https://www.adn.com/alaska-life/2020/01/19/pioneer-alaska-lawyer-dickerson-dies-at-94/, n.d., accessed 3 June 2022.

'Who was Mahala Ashley Dickerson?'; https://quakerspeak.com/video/who-was-mahala-ashley-dickerson/; April 1, 2021. accessed 4 June, 2022.

Duke University Libraries, *Guide to the Mahala Ashley Dickerson Papers, 1958-2007 and undated*, Durham, North Carolina: Duke University.

Dunbar, B. 'Black Power's Challenge to Quaker Power', *Friends Journal*, Friends Publishing Company, Philadelphia, PA, Vol. 14, No. 18, 15 September, 1968.

'Quaker Portrait: Barrington Dunbar', *Friends Journal*, Philadelphia, PA: Friends Publishing Company, 1 May, 1970.

'Fascism in the Church: Ex-Priest on "The Pope's War", Clergy Abuse and Quelling Liberation Theology', *Democracy Now!*, February 28, 2013, accessed 18 June, 2022.

Fox, M. and Griffiths, B., 'Spirituality for a New Era: Dialog with Matthew Fox and Bede Griffiths', September 1992, recorded at Holy Names College, Oakland, California.

Francis, A., 'Child Q: Met Police officers strip-search thousands of children and majority are from ethnic backgrounds', 25 March, 2022, archived at *I-news*, https://inews.co.uk/news/ child-q-met-police-strip-search-children-majority-ethnic-backgrounds-1539008, accessed 11 June, 2022.

Friends Journal article, FJ News Editors, 'William Penn's name removed from room in London's Friends House', May 5, 2021, https://www.friendsjournal.org/william-penns-name-removed-from-room-in-londons-friends-house/ accessed 14 June, 2022.

'In memoriam: H. Jack Geiger, Professor Emeritus CUNY School of Medicine and community health pioneer', ccny.cuny.edu, The City College of New York, archived at https://www.ccny.cuny. edu/news/memoriam-h-jack-geiger-professor-emeritus-cuny-school-medicine-and-community-health-pioneer, accessed 8 June, 2022.

Goldberg, S.B. (2005) 'Honoring the Unsung Heroes: Margaret Brent Awards Celebrate 15th Anniversary', American Bar Association, accessed at https://www.americanbar.org/ content/dam/aba/publishing/perspectives_magazine/women_ perspectives_HonoringUnsungHeroesSummer2005.pdf/, accessed 4 June, 2022.

Grady, D., 'H. Jack Geiger, Doctor Who Fought Social Ills, Dies at 95', *The New York Times*, December 28, 2020.

Gutierrez, G. *A Theology of Liberation*, NY: Orbis Books, 2018.

Harmon, D. (2011) 'Mahala Ashley Dickerson', *Encyclopedia of Alabama*, Alabama Humanities Foundation, accessed at http://www.encyclopediaofalabama.org/article/h-1443, accessed 4 June, 2022.

Heffer, S. (Ed.) *Great British Speeches*, London: Quercus, 2011.

Hood, James W., (Ed.) *Quakers and Literature*, Philadelphia, P.A.: Friends Association for Higher Education, 2016.

Knightley, P., Kennedy, C. *An Affair of State: The Profumo Case and the Framing of Stephen Ward*, London: Jonathan Cape, 1987.

Murgatroyd, L., 'Perhaps textile art can be a form of prophecy?', *The Friend*, Volume 178, No. 3, 17 January 2020.

National Association of Women Lawyers, "M. Ashley Dickerson Diversity Award Recipients", homepage, accessed at https://www.nawl.org/p/cm/ld/fid=71

Njuguna, N., 'On the road: journeying to becoming a Quaker diversity ally', *The Friends Quarterly*, Issue 2, 2020.

— 'Spiritual Direction from the Closet to the Marketplace', *SPIDIR Newsletter*, Autumn 2020, Edition 98.

— 'Considering Equality and Truth: Nim Njuguna Explores Three Mindsets', *The Friend*, 20 May 2021.

O'Connell, O., 'Pete Buttigieg becomes first openly gay cabinet member after historic Senate vote', *The Independent*, February 2, 2021, archived at: https://www.independent.co.uk/news/world/americas/us-politics/pete-buttigieg-openly-gay-cabinet-member-senate-b1796535.html, accessed 4 May, 2021.

Sandman, G., *Quaker Artists*, Malta, Illinois: Kishwaukee Press: 2015.

Sheehy, C. 'Profile: The larger-than-life Bishop at the centre of a scandal that rocked Ireland', *Irish Independent*, 13 March, 2017.

'Theology or Theopraxis', http://chatswithgod.com/chat/2015-01-08-theology-or-theopraxis-6042556/index.html, accessed 2 April 2022.

Vallalongo, Fred and Sally, 'Matthew Fox confronts life outside the Catholic Church', 'New Age', *The Toledo Blade*, 28 March 1993.

Watanabe, Teresa. 'Seeking the Feminine in God: Goddess worship accentuates female origins of the Almighty', *The Los Angeles Times*, November 3, 1998.

Weaver, Jr., H.D., Kriese, P. and Angell, S.W. (Eds.), *Black Fire: African American Quakers on Spirituality and Human Rights*, Philadelphia PA: QuakerPress of Friends General Conference, 2011.

Glossary

Quakers are known for using certain specific language that may be unfamiliar to non-Quakers. We use some of that language in this book plus some other specific terms which may be unfamiliar to some readers, so offer here a brief glossary for guidance to the general reader.

Allyship: A term now generally used to denote somebody who is not a member of a marginalised group, but who chooses to involve themselves in that group's work, offering their support as a relatively privileged individual, be that as an advocate, one who connects different people together, donating or raising funds, or in some other way lending moral or practical support to a cause.

FWCC: Established in 1937, Friends World Committee for Consultation works to liaise across the rich theological and cultural diversities of World Quakerism. It has its World Office at Friends House, London (Britain's central Quaker office). In addition, it has four regional sections: Africa (Regional Office, Nairobi, Kenya); Asia and West Pacific (Regional Office, Mt Lawley, Australia); Europe and Middle East (Regional Office, Birmingham, England); and the Americas (Regional Office, Philadelphia, Pennsylvania, America).

Intersectionality: This term emerged from Feminist dialectics in the 1970s in response to the layering of prejudice and abuse on individuals who partook of more than one minority characteristic. For instance, a Black gay woman would not only potentially face sexism and misogyny, but also racism and homophobia. Thus, 'intersectionality of prejudices' has been a powerful and controversial concept, used equally to upbraid White, middle-class Feminists who may have been blind to the extra challenges facing Black working-class women as much as to offer a critique of White, heteronormative, bourgeois patriarchy. More recently, the concept of 'intersectionality of prejudice' has started to be viewed as a powerful source of knowledge and experience. In this book, we also consider the potential benefit of a concept of an 'intersectionality of interests' as a means of binding together individuals and groups who might otherwise struggle to find common ground.

Meeting: This word is used by Liberal Quakers as an abbreviated version of 'Meeting for Worship' (see below), but can also refer to the worshipping community who regularly meet together for the purpose of worship, e.g., Nottingham Meeting. Some Evangelical Quakers also use this word, whilst others prefer the term 'Church'.

Meeting for Worship: A specific meeting of Quakers for the purpose of engaging in silent worship. Anyone may speak or make some other appropriate contribution (this is known as 'ministry'), but only do this when they feel genuinely inspired by 'the Spirit' (see below). Meeting for Worship generally lasts for about one hour.

Meeting House: The term generally used by Quakers for the buildings where they meet in order to worship.

Othering: The process by which individuals, groups, communities or organisations place certain types of people in the category of 'other', which in this case is a negative category, allowing for those doing the othering to exclude, mistreat and/or ignore those being 'othered'.

Quaker Faith and Practice: This is the title of Quakers' work of faith. It is an anthology of extracts from written and verbal sources through the ages up to the present day that reflect

Quaker faith, theology, and how they attempt to live out their faith, and is revised each generation. It sits alongside the Bible and other key works of faith as a vital spiritual resource.

Quakers: Members of the Religious Society of Friends, a religious movement that grew out of the religious, political and philosophical ferment of the mid-1660s. Their guiding principles include a belief in 'the Spirit', Simplicity, Truth, Equality, Peace, and Sustainability.

Religious Society of Friends (of Truth): the formal name for Quakers. Quakers often use the term 'Friend' to denote a fellow Quaker.

Silo-mentality: An unhealthily rigid, simplistic attitude and way of thinking that seeks to overtly categorise all people, concepts and things. It is summarised in the classic 'Them and Us' attitude. People who employ this mental approach may well be unable to move beyond traditional methods and understanding. Such people do not have 'fluid intelligence', the ability to think creatively in spite of divisions.

Spirit: Liberal Quakers all accept the existence of 'the Spirit', whatever that term may mean for them, which could include the Christian Trinitarian God, Unitarian God, Jewish Yahweh, Islamic Allah, Pagan spirits, a broader notion of the power of Love, and so on.

CHRISTIAN ALTERNATIVE
BOOKS

THE NEW OPEN SPACES

Throughout the two thousand years of Christian tradition
there have been, and still are, groups and individuals that
exist in the margins and upon the edge of faith. But in
Christianity's contrapuntal history it has often been these
outcasts and pioneers that have forged contemporary
orthodoxy out of former radicalism as belief evolves to engage
with and encompass the ever-changing social and scientific
realities. Real faith lies not in the comfortable certainties of
the Orthodox, but somewhere in a half-glimpsed hinterland
on the dirt track to Emmaus, where the Death of God meets
the Resurrection, where the supernatural Christ meets the
historical Jesus, and where the revolution liberates both the
oppressed and the oppressors.

Welcome to Christian Alternative... a space at the edge where
the light shines through.
If you have enjoyed this book, why not tell other readers by
posting a review on your preferred book site.

Christian Atheist
Belonging without Believing
Brian Mountford
Christian Atheists don't believe in God but miss him:
especially the transcendent beauty of his music, language,
ethics, and community.
Paperback: 978-1-84694-439-0 ebook: 978-1-84694-929-6

Compassion Or Apocalypse?
A Comprehensible Guide to the Thoughts of René Girard
James Warren
How René Girard changes the way we think about God and
the Bible, and its relevance for our apocalypse-threatened
world.
Paperback: 978-1-78279-073-0 ebook: 978-1-78279-072-3

Diary Of A Gay Priest
The Tightrope Walker
Rev. Dr. Malcolm Johnson
Full of anecdotes and amusing stories, but the Church is still a
dangerous place for a gay priest.
Paperback: 978-1-78279-002-0 ebook: 978-1-78099-999-9

Readers of ebooks can buy or view any of these bestsellers by
clicking on the live link in the title. Most titles are published
in paperback and as an ebook. Paperbacks are available in
traditional bookshops. Both print and ebook formats are
available online.

Find more titles and sign up to our readers' newsletter at
http://www.johnhuntpublishing.com/christianity Follow us on
Facebook at https://www.facebook.com/ChristianAlternative